A School
for
God's People

A HISTORY OF THE SUNDAY SCHOOL
MOVEMENT IN INDIANA

BY GROVER L. HARTMAN

CENTRAL PUBLISHING COMPANY, INC., INDIANAPOLIS,
INDIANA

Dedication

To my wife, Annabel S. Hartman, whose commitment to quality Christian education, to the education programs of the churches to which we have been related and to the Christian nurture of our family has been both inspiring and challenging to me and to our sons.

Contents

Foreword

BY ROBERT WOOD LYNN

There are few persons better qualified to tell the story of the Indiana Sunday School than Grover L. Hartman. A native Hoosier, a veteran of the Sunday School movement, and an outstanding ecumenical leader, Dr. Hartman brings to this assignment a rare combination of affection, knowledge and quiet concern. His love of his subject is especially evident in the delightful portrait of the Liberty Chapel Sunday School, where young Grover first demonstrated his flair for being a student, teacher and organization tyro. From his evocative memoir about his early days in rural Indiana to his sober (and sobering) epilogue, he leads the reader through a complex maze of events. Along the way you will discover all sorts of new persons and fresh stories. I was intrigued, for example, with the accomplishments of William H. Levering, a Lafayette businessman and a powerful leader in the heyday of the Indiana Sunday School movement in late Victorian America.

The "ups" and "downs" of the Hoosier Sunday School are faithfully recorded in these pages. A careful study of this essay will encourage all of us to think afresh of the larger meaning of the Sunday school. Grover Hartman is calling attention to the "Big Little School" as a clue to the health and vitality of the churches. As the Sunday School goes, so goes American Protestantism. If that is true, then it calls for renewed commitment at the beginning of the third century of this venerable institution.

Preface

When the Committee on the Indiana Observance of the Bicentennial of the Sunday School Movement asked me to write a history of the Sunday schools of Indiana, I was readily responsive. My own spiritual heritage is from a Hoosier Sunday school. I was nurtured in Christian experience by concerned teachers in my rural Sunday school. I believe wholeheartedly that something of the Sunday school's capacity to draw and give direction to children, to youth, and to adults must be found today or the Church will founder on the sea of secularism and indifference now surging around it. For a century and a half Sunday schools have fed the churches with young recruits. The dwindling of these nurture centers of personal religious commitment presents to the churches a major challenge for their future.

My Sunday school was in the Liberty Chapel United Brethren Church, which stood in the open country halfway between Battle Ground and Brookston in Tippecanoe County. It was a one-room frame church with a bit of a tower, from which a bell pulled by a rope below summoned the farm folks to worship and to study. Later the building was enlarged by a full basement to hold the new furnace replacing the big stove, which stood in the middle of the floor upstairs. Next to the church, when I was a boy, the remains of the one-room brick district school house reminded us that school and church had come hand in hand into Hoosierland. Across the gravel road was the cemetery where five generations of my family lie including my mother, the mentor of the Sunday school experience of my brothers and myself.

Liberty Chapel in the 1920's represented a fairly typical Indiana Sunday school, for a majority of Hoosier Sunday schools were in one-room churches with fewer than one hundred members. Certainly Liberty Chapel could not claim more than one hundred adherents. Our Sunday school attendance was about fifty. The 1920 Indiana Survey of

Religious Education found that the median Sunday school in our state had eight classes. Liberty Chapel missed that by one—unless you would count the Cradle Roll, lifted up by means of a placard on the wall listing the babies of the congregation and having attached to it by ribbons cradles representing each child.

I will never forget that Sunday school in operation at 9:30 on Sunday morning. In front, to the right of the carpeted area between the pews and the platform where stood the pulpit and the piano, was the sand table at which my mother met and loved the pre-school children. They had a few toys to play with in the sand and Mother taught with big pictures—one for each Sunday's lesson—and little picture cards with the "Golden Text" for the day, which each child was given to take home. On the third pew behind the sand table cherubs Elnora Nelson taught the primary class. Directly across the center aisle her husband, Roy, met the intermediate boys and girls using the "Youth Quarterly" from the U.B. Publishing House in Dayton, Ohio, and distributing our prized story paper, "The Friend." On the left end of the platform in pews facing the central pulpit was the older boys' class—usually pretty small—which Roy Post taught. On the other end of the platform was the "Young Ladies Class." My second cousin, Jessie Bone, who was also my first grade teacher at Battle Ground, was their popular teacher, although my father (now 95) has always made much of the fact that he was the elected teacher of that class before he and Mother were married. To complete the class offerings we had the women's class on the right in the rear and the men's class across the aisle on the left. In reflecting on the teachers I thought the women were taught by Hannah Garrott Estabrook, the wealthiest member of the congregation, who drove out from Battle Ground every Sunday to be in the old home church and whose son, Floyd, was our banker, State Senator, and landlord for the farm we share-cropped. But my dad says the teacher was Dora Grandstaff. He taught the men—in such resounding tones that all of the classes really had two lessons—their own and Father's.

x

The procedure was about the same every Sunday. My father as Superintendent called the body to order. We sang a couple of songs—rousing ones like "Bringing in the Sheaves," "Brighten the Corner Where You Are," "Rescue the Perishing," "Throw Out the Life Line," "Marching to Zion," and "Beulah Land." Then there was a prayer by someone in the school, the lesson was announced, the Golden Text read and we went to class. Roy May was our strong chorister—sometimes he sang a solo—and his wife, Effie, was pianist. The usual pattern in all the classes was to read the lesson verse by verse around the class with comments by the teacher and a minimum of discussion based on questions carried in the quarterly. In about half an hour the superintendent would pound the bell which was located on the small table in front where the secretary—usually a teen-age girl—sat. We had the secretary's report of attendance and offering, the birthday song to those who came forward to place in the miniature church bank their offering for missions equivalent to the years of their lives to date, comments on the lesson (particularly by any visitor we might have), announcements, and the closing song. The preacher, who had come out after an earlier service in Battle Ground, was given his say. I always felt sorry for him in that, customarily, about one-third of those there for Sunday school left without hearing his message.

It was my intermediate teacher, Roy Nelson, who encouraged me to make a life commitment to Christ when we had a two-week revival in the winter before I weas eleven. Soon after, John Johnson, who succeeded my father as superintendent, asked me to give my first public prayer at the opening exercises of the Sunday school. That summer the Sunday school sent me to our conference youth assembly at Oakwood Park on Lake Wawasee. I still have the notes I used in reporting that experience to the Sunday school. A year later when the Nelsons moved from their farm to West Lafayette, I—at thirteen—succeeded Roy as the intermediate teacher. I was elected president of the Christian Endeavor Society and captained a Bible Baseball team coached so well on questions from the Scriptures that we won the district championship. I can remember township Sunday school institutes—usually at Pleasant Grove south of us where J. A. Schoonover, crippled but a power in the Sunday school movement, was a member. When I was a junior in high school, I was appointed as the township representative to the Tippecanoe County United Christian Youth Council. There Ruth Fouts, the sponsor, truly became my "ecumenical mother," introducing me to the Christian youth movement in Indiana and in the nation.

I am indebted to that Sunday school—to parents who faithfully drove our carriage drawn by "Old Maude" the three miles to the church and by their example strengthened my Christian commitment; to sincere and devoted teachers; superintendents who took responsibilities for the spiritual growth of children and youth; for "saints" like Aunt Sylvia Stewart, who often began her prayers, "O God, teach us how to pray and what to pray for." Here was my start on the Christian pilgrimage.

In carrying through this historical project on the Sunday schools of Indiana, there are many to whom I am indebted. Among them are my wife and sons, who have encouraged me and helped to clear time for research and writing; Rev. Walter F. Horlander, my associate for thirteen years in the Indiana Council of Churches and coordinator of the Bicentennial Observance; the Lilly Endowment, which has financed the project, and especially Dr. Robert Lynn, its vice-president for religion, whose broad knowledge of the Sunday school movement made him a valuable counselor; Dr. Robert Steffer, visiting professor of Christian education at Christian Theological Seminary, whose critique of the manuscript in the beginning stages I appreciated greatly; the Rev. Rudy Rehmer, historian of Lutheranism in Indiana; and Dr. L. C. Rudolph, curator of the Lilly Library at Indiana University, who passed along many valuable research leads and opened to me the remarkable abstracts of the Indiana letters to the American Home Missionary Society in the first half of the Nineteenth Century. I am particularly indebted to Virginia

Dinkel, who typed the manuscript with fidelity and helpful attention to the importance of the material.

I gained a great deal from the materials and considerate staff services of the Presbyterian Historical Library in Philadelphia, which houses the archives of the American Sunday School Union, whose missionaries were a potent force in developing Sunday schools in Indiana; the collection of Sunday school materials—especially the hymnody of the movement—assembled by Dr. Lynn in the library at Union Seminary; the Archives of DePauw University and Indiana Methodism; the Mennonite Historical Library at Goshen College; the splendid collection of Baptist material at Franklin College, including the letters of that Indiana Sunday school pioneer, Jesse L. Holman; the library of Purdue University, where I had access to the excellent doctoral dissertation of David McCord on relationships of Sunday school and public school in Indiana, Herbert Heller's "Negro Education in Indiana" and Ruth Andersen's master's thesis on "Negro Education in Tippecanoe County"; the library of the Indiana State Historical Society, where I particularly benefited from manuscript materials on the beginning of the Indianapolis Sunday schools, the early Indiana newspaper files and the boxes of original American Home Missionary Society letters; and the Indiana Division of the State Library, where among many other useful resources I found the Sunday School Collection of William H. Levering, which proved to be a gold mine for information about the Sunday schools of Indiana.

If this study proves of value in interpreting the Sunday school movement in Hoosierland and in paying a deserved tribute to its leaders, I, like Paul, am debtor to many in carrying through this labor of love and profound respect.

Grover L. Hartman
March 30, 1980

Prologue

Gather thy people together, men and women, and
children, and thy stranger that is within thy gates,
that they may hear and that they may learn, and
fear the Lord your God, and observe to do all the
words of this law; and that their children which
have not known anything may hear and learn to
fear the Lord your God, as long as ye live...
Deuteronomy 31:12-13a

The 1980 bicentennial observance of the Sunday School
Movement commemorates the beginning of the Robert Raikes
Sabbath-school in Gloucester, England. There is much
evidence that the Raikes school was not actually "the first." An
English woman, Hannah Ball, gathered children of
impoverished families into her home for instruction on the
Sabbath Day as early as 1763. The chronicles of John Wesley
give support to the claim that he was teaching children on
Sunday in 1735 during his missionary sojourn in Georgia. And
it is likely that the Gloucester school was not the idea of Robert
Raikes originally but the dream of Sophia Cook, who urged
upon him the establishment of a Sabbath school for the sake of
the children of the streets—their mutual concern. Nor did
Raikes come to the Sabbath-school as a matter of religious
compulsion alone. Rather, he moved from the background of
social reform.[1]

When Robert Raikes succeeded his father as publisher of the
Gloucester *Journal* in 1857 he committed himself to jail
reform and the moral education of criminals. He followed into
their slum homes and charitable institutions the children of
the men he was trying to help in the jails and workhouses for
debtors. Many of these boys and girls worked long hours, six
days of the week in the factories springing up all over England.
On Sunday—a dirty, foul-mouthed, riotous group—they broke
forth into the streets uncontrolled and bent on mischief. They
even exploded into the countryside, leaving behind a trail of

1

disturbance and vandalism. Raikes saw a correlation between indiscipline and ignorance and crime and set about to strike a blow against crime by educating and Christianizing the children. Social control was an objective of the Gloucester school. Indeed Raikes wrote proudly to a friend: "Since the establishment of Sunday schools the children are not the ignorant creatures they were before. They have also become more tractable, and less quarrelsome and revengeful."[2] William Fox, a Baptist industrialist in London who in 1785 founded the first society for promotion of Sunday schools, set forth as his purpose: "To prevent vice, to encourage industry and virtue, to dispel the ignorance of darkness, to diffuse the light of knowledge, *to bring men cheerfully to submit to their stations*."[3]

But regardless of evidence that his school was not the first and that social motives were antecedent of the religious in his philosophy, it is not inappropriate to tie the observance of the Sunday schools' beginning to Robert Raikes and the ninety children gathered at his instigation to the Gloucester storeroom in 1780. The Sunday school "movement" in England and America stemmed from Raikes. He bore the derision of fellow citizens who branded him "Bobby Wild Goose" and scorned his "ragged regiment." He stood uncowed by the attacks of high churchmen who branded as heretical moral teaching by the four lay women he had hired. He withstood efforts in Parliament to suppress the Sunday schools. Raikes was a central figure in a movement evaluated by many as the most distinctive and influential contribution of Protestant Christianity in the English-speaking world. The Sunday schools stand beside the Wesleyan revival in that social awakening credited with saving Britain from the terrors of the French Revolution.

The Sunday School Movement spread rapidly to North America. The way had been prepared by such predecessor educational ventures of the Sunday school type as that of the German pietists at Ephrata, Pennsylvania, about 1750, Bible teaching given on the green at Washington, Connecticut, by town elders shortly after 1780, William Elliott's school in 1785 and Francis Asbury's class for the instruction of slaves in Hanover County, Virginia, in 1786.[4] *The American Sunday School Teachers' Magazine* in 1824 pointed to the New York City Sunday school of Isabella Graham and her daughter, Joanna Bethune, as the first in the United States derived from the Raikes' pattern. [5] In Philadelphia the leaders were Dr. Benjamin Rush, the famous physician and signer of the Declaration of Independence, a Unitarian layman; Matthew Carey, a Roman Catholic; and William White, the Episcopal Bishop of Pennsylvania, who had been impressed with the Sunday schools when he went to London for his consecration.[6]

Like the English sparrow, which multiplied unbelievably when brought across the Atlantic, the Sunday school thrived when introduced to the United States. Dr. D. Campbell Wyckoff of Princeton Seminary declares in picturesque style that the Sunday school is "as American as crabgrass." This ubiquitous plant, like the Sunday school a native of Europe, became widely naturalized in North America. Rooting at the joints, even in the face of constant mowing, it "makes thickset patches, a mowing merely induces new flowering and fruiting spikes that shed their prolific seed."[7].

The American compulsion to organize societies for every conceivable concern forwarded the Sunday School Movement. The husband of Joanna Bethune, a pioneer Sunday school worker, led in the establishment of the New York Sunday School Union Society, which involved male benefactors and promoters of the movement. On May 26, 1817, the Philadelphia Sunday and Adult School Union was formed. In 1821 this organization heralded the organized effort to propagate the Sunday schools by employing a missionary who within a year had organized over sixty schools in six states. In 1824 the Philadelphia society called together Sunday school leaders from other areas who established the American Sunday School Union destined to become the foremost agency in bringing Sunday schools to the West. The Union was soon yoked with two other highly significant movements created in the same period—the American Bible Society founded in 1821 and the American Tract Society launched in 1825, which before the Civil War issued 200 million books and tracts. The three provided the printed materials for the Sunday schools as they penetrated the Ohio and Mississippi Valleys.[8] With the American Home Missionary Society and state missionary societies like that in Connecticut, the American Sunday School Union provided the missionaries who must be pre-eiminently credited with carrying the network of Sunday schools to the American frontier. At its annual meeting in 1830 the American Sunday School Union in "reliance upon divine aid" resolved to establish within two years a Sunday school in every destitute place where it is practicable throughout the valley of the Mississippi." For the Union, the field stretched from Harrisburg, Pennsylvania, to the Rocky Mountains and from Canada to the Gulf of Mexico. The trumpet had sounded, summoning the faithful and concerned to the "winning of the West."[9]

CHAPTER I

Planting
Time

*Notice: The Corydon Sunday School will commence
in the Senate Chamber Sunday next at 9:00 a.m.
under superintendence of Henry B. Coburn.
Children to bring such books as they may have.*
Indiana Gazette, Corydon, Indiana,
February 3, 1820

The famous Valley Resolution of the American Sunday
School Union, envisioning as it did the propagation of Sabbath
schools in every destitute place in the West, deserves the
landmark position it has been accorded in Sunday school
history. But the pioneer Sunday schools of Indiana were not
predominantly the product of missionaries either of the Union
or of the missionary societies of the eastern seaboard. Almost
without exception they were the result of consecrated effort on
the part of Hoosier citizens—mostly lay men and lay women
who caught a vision of what Sunday schools could mean.

The theory of eastern missionary predominance in the
establishment of Indiana's first Sunday schools is long
standing. No less an authority than William H. Levering of
Lafayette, foremost Indiana Sunday school man of the last half
of the Nineteenth Century, accepted this thesis. In his

Historical Sketches of Sunday School Work[1] Levering declares:
"The first Indiana Sunday schools were not the product of the
religious enthusiasm of the pioneers. Rather they were a field
for Christian missionaries from the churches of the East—
especially New England and Philadelphia, where the Sunday
School Union was founded in 1824." Levering was in
possession of the abundant records and reports of the
American Sunday School Union in regard to its western
campaign. He goes along with the assertion of the Rev. Isaac
Reed, sent to Indiana by the Connecticut Missionary Society,
that the Sunday school he established in New Albany in April,
1819, was the first in the Hoosier State.[2] Current research
would cast doubt on this claim and credit concerned Indiana
lay folks as creators of the first Sunday schools in the new state.
In this, Indiana was like Ohio where Mrs. Mary Lake held a
Sunday school in the block house at Marietta from 1791 to
1795, the first school in Ohio and one of the first in the United
States.[3]

This denial of primary influence to New England and the
Middle Atlantic States with respect to the Sunday schools is in
keeping with the overall social, cultural and religious
development of Indiana. The flow of settlers to the Hoosier
State was from the South—Kentucky, Tennessee, North
Carolina, western Virginia—from southern Ohio and
southwestern Pennsylvania (especially after the opening of the
National Road). The Ohio River was the dominant artery for
both migration and trade.[4] As far to the North as the author's
home community, Brookston in White County seventy five
miles northwest of Indianapolis, the same migration pattern
prevailed among thirty-three families surveyed who had
settled in the area before 1860. Their former homes were:[5]

Kentucky	8	Tennessee	3	Southern Indiana	1
Ohio	8	North Carolina	2		
Virginia	8	West Virginia	2		

Aside from the predominance of the Ohio River as a
transportation factor, the major reason for the lack of New

England and Middle Atlantic influence was the all but impenetrable swamps in the northeastern part of the state and in the Kankakee River Valley.[6] Passing through the latter area in 1853 on one of the first trains of the Monon Railroad, Horace Greeley declared that, had John Bunyan seen the Kankakee marshes, he could have improved on his description of the Slough of Despond in *Pilgrim's Progress*.[7] Confronted by the swamps, Easterners tended to bypass Indiana following the shore of Lake Michigan to more inviting lands in Michigan and Illinois. Rooted in this overwhelming southern influence are the antipathy to New England and eastern ways reflected in the plaintive letters of representatives of the missionary societies, the strength of the Copperheads (Southern sympathizers in the Civil War era) and the power of the Ku Klux Klan in Indiana in the 1920's.

The Sunday School Pioneers

As we turn to the founding of the early Indiana Sunday schools, it is to be noted that the Rev. Adam Condo in his *History of the Indiana Conference of the United Brethren in Christ* claims the honor of starting the first Hoosier Sunday school for the versatile physician and preacher of the UB church Dr. John George Pfrimmer.[8] Condo places the school at Corydon as early as 1814. Pfrimmer is certainly worthy of high ranking as a Sunday school man. Born in Alsace, trained in medicine and for a time a physician and surgeon in the French navy, Pfrimmer came to the United States in 1783. He was converted in 1790 and began preaching immediately. Bishop Christian Newcomer, successor of Phillip William Otterbein in the episcopal office, visited John George Pfrimmer at his home in Ohio. The Bishop wrote that he "came to Brother Pfrimmer's on May 21, 1800. About 30 children had assembled at his house, to whom he was giving religious instruction". Dr. Pfrimmer moved to Harrison County, Indiana, and entered land near Corydon in 1808. He organized the first United

Brethern Church in Indiana in 1812 known as Pfrimmer's Chapel. In 1813 he organized the Stonecypher Church 3½ miles southeast of Corydon and a church among the German people who had arrived in Charlestown near New Albany. Early in 1814 Pfrimmer started the Corydon Church and, knowing his devotion to the Sunday school idea, Condo believes he started a Sunday school in Corydon as early as 1814. Besides medicine, preaching and farming his Harrison County land, Pfrimmer was active in establishing county government and in building the old State House. He was appointed a probate judge by William Henry Harrison, the territorial Governor, who was also his business partner. In addition, he was an accomplished musician bringing to Corydon what is believed to be the first piano in Indiana.

Dr. Henry Little, for more than sixty years connected with Sunday schools in Indiana, in an address to the Indiana Sunday School Association in 1879, asserted that there was a thriving Sunday school in Madison in 1816.[9] "Godly women", said Dr. Little, "went around amongst the poor and friendless little boys and girls, got them to promise to come to the school and then provided them with decent clothing so they might come together. They were not looking after children of church members but hunting up neglected ones." A young woman whom Dr. Little knew met a bright looking boy on the street. She found that he could not read, that his brothers couldn't read and he named off six boys in the neighborhood who couldn't read either. The woman invited the lads to her Sunday school in a room where she taught a private school during the week. There she taught them to read and write. Thus it was nameless "godly women" who started what may have been Indiana's second Sunday school.

The Rev. Isaac Reed and his New Albany school are not to be overlooked. Reed's book, *The Christian Traveller*, stands as a revealing record of life in early Indiana and of the spread of Christianity in the Middle West via the circuit riders. Reed was a product of Middlebury College in Vermont, was under care of Long Island Presbytery in New York and was licensed

Isaac Coe, M.D.

The Rev. Isaac Reed

Jesse L. Holman

John George Pfrimmer, M.D.

The Rev. Ransom Hawley

Sarah Hall Hawley

by the Fairfield Congregational Association in Connecticut. Although coming West as a Congregationalist, Reed, during his forty years in Indiana, founded more churches than any other eastern missionary—all of them Presbyterian in keeping with the 1801 Congregational-Presbyterian compact for the evangelization of the West. In one year—1824—he rode 2480 miles on horseback going as far west as Missouri. Ordained by Transylvania Presbytery on October 10, 1818, Reed in the same month crossed the Ohio River to become one of the first "settled" ministers in Indiana at New Albany where the fifteen member Presbyterian congregation promised him a salary of $500 a year. Laid out in 1813, New Albany by 1818 had become Indiana's largest town with 700 population and such commercial advances as a steam saw mill, several stores, mechanics shops and a boat yard to build steam boats. The trunks of large trees, felled but not cleared, lay around town. There was no church building of any kind. Out of the community Reed gathered in the "miserable log school house" a Sunday school of sixty members which he described as "the first ever formed in Indiana."[10]

The founder of the first Sunday school in Indianapolis was Dr. Isaac Coe, a native of Morris County, New Jersey, who grew up in Herkimer County, New York. He was graduated in medicine and surgery from the New York Medical Institution and Hospital in New York City and after six years practicing in New Jersey and Virginia came to Indianapolis in 1821, the first graduate physician in the new city. The enterprising young doctor started an adult Bible class in his home in February, 1822, and began the Indianapolis Sunday school in April a year later. The announcement of the school which appeared in the Indianapolis *Gazette*, April 5, 1823, is an interesting one—"The Indianapolis Sabbath School will commence on next Sabbath the sixth day of April inst. at 9:00 in the morning at Mr. C. Scudder's shop. A general and punctual attendance of scholars is requested, and that they bring with them the Testaments, spelling books or such other books as they may have."[11] Here again, a layman was the pioneer. The setting was non-churchly and the educational focus was general.

When the American Sunday School Union adopted its famous Valley Resolution in May, 1830, one in Philadelphia voting for it as a new vice-president of the Board was a Hoosier from Aurora in Dearborn County, Jesse L. Holman. By the early 1830's, Holman had created a Sunday school union in his own area—one of the first in the West to affiliate with the Philadelphia body. The southeastern Indiana union reported 20 schools, 1,200 scholars and 200 teachers.[12] Converted at seventeen by Baptists in northern Kentucky, Holman trained in law and came to Indiana in 1811 at the age of 28. William Henry Harrison made him district attorney for Dearborn and Jefferson Counties. He was elected to the Territorial Legislature and for two years was presiding judge in his district. With statehood in 1816 he was appointed to the State Supreme Court, serving fourteen years. In 1831 he missed by one vote election to the United States Senate. In 1835 he was appointed federal judge for Indiana and served until his death in 1842. As early as 1825 one of the American Home Missionary Society preachers described the strong Sunday school in Aurora with Holman as the leader. He continued as a vice-president of the American Sunday School Union for twelve years being succeeded there by Dr. Isaac Coe of Indianapolis. Interested in the distribution of religious books and tracts, he became president of the Western Publishing and Sunday School Society, which he had helped to establish in Cincinnati. Holman was also one of the leading supporters and money raisers for Isaac McCoy's mission to the Indians of northern Indiana and later in Kansas.[13]

Another early focus for Sunday school development was in Davies County in southwestern Indiana. There the leaders were a husband and wife team, Ransom and Sarah Hawley. Both were born in Connecticut in 1802. The Rev. Mr. Hawley came to Washington in Davies County as a missionary immediately after his graduation from Auburn Theological Seminary in 1828. He was married in 1830 and thereafter his wife was a zealous co-worker in his ministry of sixty-one years which, according to his records, included the delivery of 6,350 sermons, the receiving of 540 persons into church membership, 400 baptisms, the organization of four churches, the building of five houses of worship, 370 marriages, the distribution of more than 1,000 Bibles and 30,000 tracts and 90,000 miles of travel on horseback. Hawley founded a number of Sunday schools and in 1829, according to the Washington *Evening Gazette*, established the Davies County Sunday School Union, which William Levering labeled as the first such union in Indiana, although this honor might be disputed by the Holman advocates and those who back the Sabbath School Union Society said to have been organized at Charlestown in October, 1825.[14]

Indication of the spread of Sunday schools comes in the record of the first such school in Lake County, the most northwestern of Indiana's counties adjacent to Chicago. There the first settlement was in the Pleasant Grove area where Ephraim Bryant arrived in 1837. By 1840, three Sunday schools were serving in that section of the county.[15]

The movement had its martyrs. The 1830 annual report of the American Sunday School Union told of the death of one of the Sunday school missionaries who started from Springfield, Illinois, to the Wabash on January 12. The family with whom he stayed on the night of the 18th urged him to wait a day because of the intense cold. There were ahead of him two windswept prairies—one of 12 miles, the other of 17 miles—and two forks of the Kaskaskia River before he could reach shelter. He was found dead in the waters of the Big Okaw only a few miles from his destination.

The Launching Process—Supporters and Opponents

Whether the organizer of an Indiana Sunday school was an eastern missionary or a concerned local resident, the development pattern was fairly consistent. Isaac Reed went from house to house; the "godly women" who led out in Madison talked to children on the streets; in Corydon and Indianapolis, newspaper notices were utilized. The Sunday school people saw illiteracy and ignorance on every hand. Reed stopped at a hut "where there was a hearty man, his wife and four plump but dirty children. They were without chairs, and, what is more, without a Bible, and they scarcely ever heard preaching. The man can read a little, his wife not at all and there is no school for the children."[16] Letter after letter to the American Home Missionary Society gave proof that Indiana was indeed a destitute place. Many communities in the 1820's and 1830's— and even later—had no public schools and, if they did, these pioneer institutions were often set up in shacks, with inferior teachers and on the basis of extremely short terms. In area after area, the Sunday schools were the first educational ventures and their libraries—always part of a Sunday school, however humble—contained most of the books the communities could muster.

Yet the Sunday schools were not received with open arms. Isaac Reed recounts the active opposition of some Baptist preachers who, possessed of no formal education themselves, saw little need of it for others. Reed declared that these frontier preachers "have neither the knowledge, order nor apparent piety of the Baptists in northern states."[17] A bitter attack upon the Methodist preachers in Elkhart County was made by Noah Cooke in a letter to the American Home Missionary Society in 1833.[18] Said Cooke, "The greatest obstacle there to the cause of vital piety is Methodism." The Methodist preachers came to preach, not to teach. They spoke the language of the people and didn't push them toward book learning like the Presbyterians. Peter Cartwright said of the Western Conference that in 1820-21 there were 280 circuit riders and that among these itinerants there was not one literary man.[19]

Children themselves did not always welcome these invasions of their carefree and blissfully ignorant lives. One of the original members of the Indianapolis union school, looking back after fifty years on his experience, wrote: "Fifty years ago

I entered that school a boy eight years old, and did not know one letter of the alphabet, nor do I believe that among the ten or twelve boys present there was one who could spell his own name, or would know it should he see it in print. The Sunday school had been the topic of conversation with the boys of the village for some time. We thought it a great imposition upon our personal rights. We thought that Messrs. Coe, Blake, and Ray, who organized the school were assuming power they had no right to."[20]

Often there was widespread community hostility to any interference with Sabbath relaxation, including drinking. One upright farmer, approached by Reed to join in the call to worship services and a Sabbath school, said he couldn't afford to sign a notice but he would put it up at the neighborhood still where everybody would see it.[21] John J. Funk, one of the leaders in the development of Sunday schools among the Mennonites, declared, "Sunday schools in the early days of my life were not only considered needless to the development of the Christian life and church prosperity but were looked upon as an innovation that was absolutely detrimental to the promotion of an humble, devoted Christian life and the advancement of religious devotion; and above all that it was an open door to lead children and young people into wordliness, vanity and pride."[22] Funk agreed that Sunday schools would overcome the religious illiteracy and indifference threatening society, that they would eliminate Sabbath desecration, foster worship and reverence, facilitate evangelism and nurture the spiritual life. Critics struck back declaring there was no Scripture command for such an organization, no Scripture base for lay persons teaching publicly, that it was a violation of Scripture to allow women to teach, that it was unscriptural to allow non-Mennonites to teach in a Mennonite church, that Sunday schools were being promoted by the highest, proudest and dressiest classes in the country and to follow them was to conform to the world. It was further asserted that Sunday schools used other books than God's word and some were not opposed to war, bloodshed and lawsuits, that they fostered pride and exaltedness by giving the most progressive scholars prizes and marks of honor and that they had banished the Bible from weekday schools, thus giving Satan a greater scope of operation.

Among the Disciples of Christ—usually cited as "the Campbellites" in pioneer Indiana—there was considerable distrust of the Sunday schools. Alexander Campbell in 1823 voiced opposition to societies in the church on the grounds that they did not exist in New Testament churches. He viewed Sunday schools as recruiting establishments to fill the ranks of sects.[23] Campbell believed that religious education was a function of the family and that it was to be approached through personal Bible study. Barton Stone held similar views, but both men found appealing the nondenominational character of the Sunday schools. Some Disciples saw the Sunday schools as a human effort for the conversion of men, a presumptuous attempt to aid God in a work that belonged to Him alone. Elijah Goodwin, leader in religious education among the Christian churches, recognized more persuasive criticisms— poorly conducted schools, inadequate literature and teachers and officers short on training for their roles.[24]

In spite of these barriers of inertia and forthright opposition, the Sunday schools prevailed. Sometimes, as among the Mennonites and German Lutherans, they were sold as a means to teach the German language, which the children were losing in the English-speaking public schools.[25] But more often the Sunday schools won out by means of spiritual claims and the high level commitment of their proponents. In spite of opposition, the fifth annual report of the American Sunday School Union in 1829 recorded 100 Sunday schools in Indiana with 741 teachers and 5,651 scholars. The interesting thing is that a majority of these schools were sponsored by the Methodists. The church in the West was evidently catching up with the directive of the famous Christmas Conference of 1784 which launched Methodism as an independent church in the new United States of America. That conference answered a query—"What shall we do for the rising generation?" by declaring: "When there are ten children whose parents are in society meet them at least an hour every week, talk with them at home and pray in earnest for them."[26]

The Early Sunday School at Work

There are extant some first-hand accounts of early Indiana Sunday schools in operation. One of the most interesting is James M. Ray's paper on "First Sunday School Efforts in Indianapolis" delivered at closing exercises of the Sunday school at First Presbyterian Church on April 1, 1866, and reproduced in the "Centennial Memorial" of that church published in 1923. Ray was the son-in-law of Dr. Isaac Coe, founder of the Indianapolis school, who also brought about his conversion.* Ray relates that the early settlers in Indianapolis

James M. Ray

_____

*Ray, a native of New Jersey, whose life stretched from 1800 to 1881, came to Indianapolis from Kentucky in the fall of 1821. He was elected clerk of Marion County in 1831, serving until 1834 when he became cashier of the State Bank. A memorial at the State Sunday School Convention at the time of his death described Ray as "quiet, unobtrusive, vigilant, never careless, never idle, highly regarded and trusted." His community services included secretary/business manager of a variety of organizations from town meetings to the fire company and missionary society.

were caught up with the prospect that their city was soon to be the State's capital and that there was among them widespread recognition of the need for moral and religious influence. At that time, according to Ray, the people enjoyed only an occasional sermon by a traveling preacher and "there was not much to distinguish the Sabbath from any other day."

The voluminous letters of the representatives in Indiana of both the American Sunday School Union and the American Home Missionary Society reveal how generally Sunday schools preceded churches in bringing religion to frontier communities. The idea of a Sunday school was well received when advanced by Dr. Coe, who "was entirely alone in having knowledge or experience in the formation of Sabbath schools." Experience with the concept was gained in the "Bible school for grown persons" inaugurated by Dr. Coe on February 22, 1822. This school met every other Sunday morning at 9:00 at the home of Lismund Basye, "a devoted Methodist brother." They elected a first superintendent, a second superintendent, a secretary, assistant secretary and treasurer. The superintendents with Dr. Coe, James Blake and Judge McIlwain constituted a committee to select questions to be proved by Scripture. Such questions were a standard aspect of the operating procedure in the schools for children as well as adults. A total of 34, including "a number of ladies," enrolled in the adult school, which ran until fall when "nearly universal sickness consumed the time of all as nurses or patients."

On March 22, 1823, a meeting was held at the school house to consider formation of a "Presbyterian Society." The same night a committee was set up to meet the following Thursday evening "to organize a Sunday school." The union or interdenominational basis* for the school (characteristic of the

---

*William Levering, historian of the Indiana Sunday schools reflected this principle when he wrote in *The Awakener* of July, 1902: "The church member who has not grown tall enough to see over his denominational fence needs to borrow our interdenominational step ladder and take a peep at his neighbor."

frontier Sunday schools generally) was affirmed in the membership of the committee—Dr. Coe and the organizing pastor of the Presbyterian Society, David C. Proctor; Lismund Basye, a Methodist; John McClung, a Campbellite; and John Hawkins, a Baptist. The committee worked quickly and had its notice in the *Gazette* on April 5 announcing the first session of the school the following day at 9:00 in Caleb Scudder's cabinet shop. Besides cheerfully preparing his shop each Saturday afternoon for the Sunday school, Scudder became a teacher and later superintendent of the school. James Ray refers to him as "the sweet singer who led all our songs of public praise for many years."

Thirty scholars came to Scudder's shop for the first meeting of the new school. Within three weeks the number had risen to 70. During the first year a total of 98 enrolled and the average attendance was 40. In 1824 the average attendance was 56. In the third year a canvass of the town revealed approximately 200 children of school age. By the end of the year, 161 had been enrolled in the Sunday school and the average attendance had climbed to 75. It was estimated the one-fourth of the children came from outside the "city" limits, some traveling from two to five miles.

Other Sunday schools soon appeared. In 1828 Wesley Chapel—the first Methodist society worshiping in a log church just south of the present Monument Circle—opened a school, which, in its second year, enrolled 176 children and reported an average attendance of 92. The Baptists followed in November, 1833, with a school which the next year had on roll 100 scholars and averaged 60 in attendance. The first Episcopal school was begun in 1837, but James Ray had no statistics for it. The English Lutheran congregation inaugurated its Sunday school on July 6, 1839, and in its first year enrolled 37 scholars and maintained an average attendance of 20. The Second Presbyterian Church launched a school in August, 1839, which, during 1840, enrolled 50 and had an average attendance of 31. Roberts Chapel, the second Methodist church, entered the Sunday school field in

December 1842 and a year later reported 120 scholars and attendance averaging 80. The Christian Reformed Church began Sunday school work in 1843, and by the onslaught of the Civil War there was a school connected with every Christian denomination in town.

A cooperative venture of six Indianapolis Sunday schools was a system of monthly visiting to homes of the community first undertaken in 1836. At the end of that year, of 558 eligible children, 430—77%—were enrolled in Sunday school. The program was continued and by 1846 nine out of ten children—90% of 1,206—were on the Sunday school rolls.

A similar record of the beginnings of the Greencastle Sunday school has been preserved.[27] This, too, was a union school begun on the second Sunday in April 1834 by the teacher of the day school for the benefit of her pupils. This woman taught the school alone until increased enrollment led her to call in friends to help. By the end of June the school had 50 scholars and had elected a president, vice-president, superintendent, secretary, librarian and six teachers. By November 10 the enrollment had climbed to 80—53 girls and 27 boys. There were four male and five female teachers and six professors of religion. The latter, who show up in other early schools, were responsible for religious instruction and examination of the children for religious growth, supplementing the teachers who worked on writing, spelling and reading as well as religious teaching. The school convened at 9:00 a.m. each Sunday.

During its first year, the Greencastle school received $5.00 from a "Sabbath school" in Pepperell, Massachusetts, to aid in purchasing books. The American Sunday School Union added $5.00 and $4.50 was raised by townspeople. Through these gifts a library of 70 volumes was assembled from which scholars able to read were allowed to take out one book a week to be returned the following Sunday. Teachers' meetings were held weekly to examine the lessons and to prepare mutually for them. The Union Questions (from the American Sunday School Union), like those developed in the Indianapolis school, added interest. There was a Sunday school concert on the second Monday of each month. Special mention was made of the fact that the school—unlike many others on the frontier—was to continue throughout the winter. It is noteworthy, too, that in the first year of the school's operation no Sunday school agent and only one preacher visited it. The reporter closed by writing: "Though we cannot tell of many souls converted, or discover any special seriousness, yet we sow in hope that the Holy Spirit will shed its gentle dews on these young hearts, and that they will be renewed by its heavenly influences."

One of the first of the Mennonite Sunday schools in Kosciusko County near the Michigan border was described in a letter to that denomination's national publication, the *Herald of Truth*[28]:

The brethren here during the summer had organized a Sunday school which met every time they had meeting at nine o'clock in the morning and continued until ten, at which time the meeting begins. This was the closing day for the season, and each scholar received a small book or a card as a present. The school is closed during the winter months for the reason that it is impracticable to keep it open when those attending live so far from each other. The school was instituted for the purpose of instructing the children and youth in the truths of the Bible and in their duty to God and man, and to lead them betimes in wisdom's way. It was truly encouraging to my heart as I sat there and saw the children and young men and women sitting together there reading the word of God and receiving instruction from its precious precepts. I thought of the hundreds and the thousands who spend their precious Sabbath hours in idleness—in sinful pleasures and wicked associations, and have no regard for the commandments of the Lord and the precepts of His word. How much better a portion have they chosen who go where Christians meet to teach them, and learn the way of life, than those who walk in the counsels of the ungodly.

Returning to the Indianapolis Union School, James Ray recorded that rewards for memorizing were a feature of the program. The extent of memorization is unbelievable to present-day educators. Archibald Craig, an American Home

Missionary Society representative, in Franklin County (southeastern Indiana) in a letter of August 14, 1830, reported that in one of his schools 200 to 300 verses were recited each Sunday and that within two months 12,000 verses had been memorized.[29] Many scholars "learned by heart" all four Gospels and one boy was said to have memorized the entire Bible from Genesis to Revelation. In the Indianapolis school, one verse of Scripture, four paragraphs or stanzas in reading, or mastery of ten spelling words brought a "book credit" of one cent. Since some tracts could be purchased for ½¢ or a penny and the American Sunday School Union in this period sold simple books at 6¼¢, a youngster could soon build up a respectable family library; and the value of this program in providing reading materials to the frontier is not to be underestimated. The scarcity of common school education (reflected in the complete illiteracy of many boys in the school noted earlier) made it necessary to begin with the rudiments among the younger scholars on whom, as well as on the more advanced scholars, the gifts of attractive books (as James Ray saw it) had a marked influence in securing diligence and perseverance in study. Concern about the rewards system and the attendant costs led to its termination in 1831. It had been found in promoting the Sunday school that many were prejudiced against any "system of distinction."

Some reluctant parents charged that Sunday school men received salaries for their services and commissions on the children enrolled. Worse yet, it was said that rolls were sent to England with every scholar becoming thereby a subject of the British King. The leaders were accused of profiting from the sale of books to the children. The recurring charge of "sectarianism" was refuted by the declaration that teaching positions and enrollment were open to "all, who, in evangelical faith, would work together in love." When the population of Indianapolis reached 3,000, the number of teachers and officers in the Sunday schools had risen to 1,000—one-third of the population—and there were 140 teachers and officers. In 1829, two Sunday school men—a Baptist and a Presbyterian—

Record card (upper) and certificate of dismissal (lower) issued by the American Sunday School Union, the record card bearing at lower edge, the imprint of that organization. These cards were used in the Union Sabbath School later known as The Sunday School attached to the First Presbyterian Church.

Record card is dated 1832 and is signed by Isaac Coe and Caleb Scudder, the one the religious instructor, the other the teacher of the class.

Dismissal card carries the signature of Governor Samuel Bigger, teacher, and is dated October 31, 1841.

American Sunday School Union Record Forms

were appointed to organize other schools and this "home missionary" effort led to the establishment of twenty schools in Marion (where Indianapolis is located), Hendricks, and Morgan Counties.

In October 1825, the Sabbath School Union Society was organized in a meeting at Charlestown in Clark County on the Ohio River. The organizers had record of 2,000 children in Sabbath schools, but lamented over the 48,000 who were not attending, many of whom "are growing up in great ignorance, and thus preparing for great wickedness."[30] The president of this first state society was Judge James Scott of the State Supreme Court, who had authored the famous Ninth Article of the Constitution of 1816, covering education, charities, corrections, and public libraries. Judge Jeremiah Sullivan was one of three vice-presidents and Dr. Isaac Coe was one of eleven elected to the Board of Managers. One of the actions of the Society was to create a Committee on Publication to "address the public with full directions for organizing and conducting Sunday schools." This Committee's publication is a memorable formulation of the pattern for early Indiana Sunday schools. Among its directives were the following:[31]

Superintendents—four if over 100 (never less than two); one to take government of the school, assign teachers to classes, see that each class has a teacher; the second to examine and classify scholars, see that they have proper books of which he keeps account; the third to keep the records of the school; and the fourth to examine the performance of the teachers and instruct them as necessary.

Teachers—one to each class and a substitute if possible.

Scholars — all capable of learning admitted and continued if they behave well. Early enrollment is encouraged.

Classification—(1) those who study the Scriptures; (2) those who memorize hymns and catechisms; (3) those who spell in two or more syllables; (4) those who are learning the alphabet and monosyllables. Divide classes into groups of 6 to 12; reclassify quarterly.

Books—The first class should memorize Matthew beginning at the second chapter, John, Acts, and Romans, plus selections from Genesis, Exodus, Deuteronomy, and elsewhere in the Bible as determined. Catechisms and hymns are to be those published by the American Sunday School Union prepared by a committee from the principal religious denominations and contain no doctrines in which all do not unite. In Indianapolis, Watt's *First Catechism, Milk for Babes*, Watt's *Divine and Moral Songs*, Doddridge's *Poetical Lessons*, and *Taylor's Original Hymns* are learned. Third class—a spelling book; fourth class—the *Sunday School Spelling Book*, the *Union Primer*, or Webster's *Spelling Book*.

The policy is to provide books which students will buy through their earnings [for memorization].

Remarks—Rewards are believed necessary to secure punctuality and stimulate to industry during the week; to place before human nature some motive to induce exertion. To this end, books, use of the library, distinction in school, and the approbation of teachers are elements.

Library Regulations—Books shall be classified in range from 12¢ and under to $2.00. Scholars after attendance of one month and having a good record in their instruction shall be entitled to draw a book from the library according to the value attached monetarily to their performance in class. . . . Every dirt or grease spot, turned down or torn page, or failure to return book on time shall result in a fine of 1¢ to 7¢ according to the class of the book. A lost book shall be paid for in money or through the credits from memorizing. Books should be issued weekly before the close of school, and officers and teachers may borrow subject to the same regulations as the children.

The Committee closed its publication with an address to the public which called for enlistment in "this blessed cause". . . . "Hold out to the end; and you may hope at last to see some of the dear pupils whom you have taught or enabled others to teach, forming a part of your crown of rejoicing in the day of the Lord Jesus."[32]

James Ray declared that the unity achieved in the Sunday school carried over to the facing of other concerns advancing every moral and religious enterprise. He particularly marked the importance of the united canvass of families and the union prayer meeting on the second Monday night of each month.

It is clear that the Indianapolis Sunday schools drew to them top community leaders. Noteworthy among these was Calvin Fletcher, generally regarded as the first citizen of early Indianapolis and certainly by record the top taxpayer in the young city. The six-volume diary of this remarkable leader, which carefully reports many community services, records his story as a "Sunday school man."[33] Born in Vermont in 1798, Fletcher moved to Urbana, Ohio, in 1817 where he read law and came to Indianapolis in September 1821 soon after his marriage. Although he arrived virtually penniless, he became a highly successful lawyer, banker, and farm operator. He served seven years in the state senate and is remembered for his advocacy of free public schools, his championing of the anti-slavery movement and his role in organizing agricultural fairs. Deeply religious and possessed of noteworthy intellectual curiosity, Fletcher was drawn into the Methodist Sunday school and carried his eleven children—nine sons and two daughters—with him into it.

On March 15, 1840, Rev. Allen Wiley and wife, dinner guests of the Fletchers, urged their host "to take part in the M.E. Sunday school." Fletcher said, "No"; but, when notified on April 15 that he had been appointed a teacher, he accepted, recording: "Up to this time I have not taken any part in the school. It is understood it is going down. It has been reorganized. I have been repeatedly solicited to take a part in the school and have not yielded to such solicitation without many groans and scruples. I hope I may be useful."

In April, 1841, Fletcher attended the election of superintendents of the Sunday school and on March 30, 1842, went "to Mr. Wilkins to meet managers of the Sabbath school. We made out a list of sixteen male and fifteen female teachers and six teachers of Bible classes." The election of his son, Elijah, as secretary of the school pleased Fletcher and occasioned the recording of his own philosophy of service (April 2, 1842): "I do not ask any high office or low; yet if a humble one is offered, I make it a rule to serve with zeal and diligence; but when my time expires to retire and leave it for others but to leave if possible the office with credit—dignify the office and not suppose the office is to dignify me."

At the "Sabbath School" election of 1842, Fletcher became one of the superintendents along with two other men and two women. His diary notes pertaining to fulfillment of this responsibility are numerous and revealing of the nature of the Sunday school movement in his day:

April 20, 1842—one of the superintendents absent at the colored school.*

July 4—1,200 to 1,500 Sunday school scholars paraded: more girls than boys. John Ray had care of colored children—20 to 30.

---

*A Methodist Society of Negroes was organized in 1836, which became Bethel African Methodist Episcopal Church.

September 27—lectured on 11th and 12th chapters of Acts and made comments on the subject of theaters. Two boys had 100 verses. School has lessened in numbers but improved in attention....To examine character of Barach and Deborah in Judges next Sunday.

January 10, 1843—examined on character of Elisha. From ignorance and bad habits already acquired of teachers and children I fear the Sabbath schools can't flourish, can't exist.

Fourth of July—200 M.E. Sabbath school children with scholars from the Episcopal, Baptist, and Presbyterian schools (a total of 800) marched led by Marion Guards. Children, marshalled at 6:30 in morning, marched to grove south of town where joined by 800 or more adults. I was one hour in delivering my address during which good order prevailed.

June 28, 1845—addressed colored Sabbath school [in a small frame meeting house on the north side of Georgia Street between Senate and the canal which Fletcher had helped the congregation to build].

October 5, 1851—went to Baptist and Christian Sunday schools in the morning and the two Presbyterian churches at night urging them to attend the 25th anniversary celebration of the Sabbath school union of the ME Church on Thursday, October 9. [On that date the schools assembled and marched to the Masonic Hall which was filled for the two anniversary addresses.]

1857—active in preparing for and attending the first Indiana Sabbath School Convention.

April 10, 1859—Sabbath Schools had anniversary. I did not attend but probably should have done so. I am avoiding all official stations in Church and State. I can't exercise them without great pain and anxiety. I feel that others should exercise them but what is painful I see many make displays in these matters that are dishonest and refuse to perform the duties of life one with another. This discourages me. Many do all their public religious acts to be seen of men, have no heart in the cause of benevolence, do as little as they can and never or rarely do anything unless it come to public notice. Such men I cannot well associate with in public matters—especially of a religious nature.

Before Fletcher laid down his responsibilities, another noted man had entered the Sunday school scene. Benjamin Harrison, future president of the United States, had arrived in Indianapolis with his young bride in 1854.[34] Harrison quickly affiliated with First Presbyterian Church, which was carrying forward what had been the Union Sunday School of 1823. The session record states:

When he came to this place in 1854 at the age of 21 he lost no time in uniting with this church and taking up such work as he found to do. He became a teacher in the Sabbath School and was constant in his attendance on church services; his voice was heard in prayer meetings; he labored for and with young men especially in the YMCA. And in whatever way opened, whether public or private, he gave testimony for his faith and the lordship of his Master.[35]

By the time he departed for military service in the Civil War, young Harrison was superintendent of the First Presbyterian Sunday school and Mrs. Harrison had charge of the infants' department.[36] With this background on the part of the newly elected President, one can understand his affirmative response to the Philadelphia merchant, John Wanamaker, who, on being asked to become Postmaster General, accepted with the proviso that he might return on weekends to the superintendency of his Bethany Sunday school, widely regarded as the greatest Sunday school in the land.[37]

Among other big guns drawn up in support of Sunday schools was the eloquent and influential Henry Ward Beecher. The great preacher, orator, and reformer has recorded his support of Sunday schools during his early pastorate at Lawrenceburg in the Dearborn County domain of Jesse L. Holman. He continued to speak out for the schools during his period of service at Second Presbyterian Church in Indianapolis.[38] Beecher drew upon his Indiana experience when in 1848 he came from his Brooklyn Church to the 24th annual meeting of the American Sunday School Union championing a resolution which declared:

"That the American Sunday School Union, securing as it does the concurrence and sympathy of Christians of various denominations, and connecting the establishment of schools with the distribution of appropriate books for children and youth, possess means for influencing the generations of the

West, which the Church and the country cannot too highly appreciate, nor too vigorously employ."

Hoosiers are indebted to a British Quaker for the most complete description of an Indiana Sunday school in operation which has come to light. After traveling over the United States, William Tallack published his *Friendly Sketches in America*, in which he reported visits to "First Day Schools."[39] Near the end of the decade which preceded the Civil War, Tallack came to Richmond, Indiana, and visited the Richmond school, whose inspiring superintendent was Elijah Coffin, cashier of the National Bank. The school convened in the large meeting house from 9:00 to 10:45 a.m., just ahead of the First Day Meeting for worship. The British visitor found seventeen classes in session with 130 scholars. The oldest grouping—"the spectacled class"—consisting of twenty elderly women was gathered in the gallery reading in slow-paced style from the Sixth Chapter of Revelation with a male Friends minister as teacher. A class of young men was taught by an "intelligent Friend" with a Greek New Testament in hand for reference. Across the room another class of ten youths was considering an historical question and the teacher was using *Adam Clark's Commentary* to elucidate the subject. At the other end of the room, the clerk of the Indiana Yearly Meeting (also a banker) guided fifteen young women into examination of the resurrection and the future state, employing many references to raising from the dead.

In the corner, a class of six older men was engaged with the Transfiguration. Theirs was a case of mutual instruction without a teacher. In another area of the meeting house were several classes for girls of various ages. Another for still younger girls and taught by the wife of the man leading the young women's class was also studying the resurrection and reciting many memorized verses assigned the week before.

At the far end of the room was the infant class taught by a cheerful female using pictures with children too young to read. The lesson being on Noah's Ark, one child asked, "Were there fish on the ark?" to which the teacher promptly replied, "Yes, as food." Across the room a small class of four boys evinced strong interest in Jonah and the whale.

In most of the classes the lesson was read verse by verse all around, followed by questions and comparisons with parallel passages. In use with the children were "Mother's Catechism" and "Questions on Luke and John," compiled by Superintendent Coffin. Some Biblical cyclopedias and dictionaries were in evidence.

Tallack found that about four-fifths of the 130 in attendance were Friends. The whole school was assembled ten minutes before dismissal so that selected individuals picked by the superintendent as he moved about the school could recite their memorized verses. Visitors were invited to address the children, and two Methodists present—a young minister and a layman from a church out of town—responded. The whole morning, said Tallack, was "a pleasant, cheerful, and very interesting one." He found First Day Schools in nearly all the meetings belonging to the Indiana and Western Yearly Meetings, the latter being headquartered at Plainfield west of Indianapolis.

Curriculum Materials and Hymnody

The provision of materials for the Sunday schools and for the inspiration of the scholars was a huge task in itself. In its first year, the American Sunday School Union reported publication of 1,082,650 units[40] including:

42,500 reward books	10,000 spelling books
51,000 tracts	726,000 memorization tickets
10,000 Decalogue	25,000 hymn books
500 minute books	1,000 "Plan of Proceeding"
4,000 catechisms	2,000 hymns on sheets
10,000 Christian Almanac	650 receiving books
11,000 alphabetical cards	3,500 annual reports

By 1846, book sales, according to the Annual Report, had climbed to $84,443. It is to be noted how practically relevant these publications were—organizational guides, minute books, catechisms (as noted above used in the Indianapolis Union School along with hymns as the curriculum for one class level), tickets given to children in recognition of memorized verses, and the coveted reward books and tracts.

The questions designed for use in opening up the Scriptures represented another need. Dr. Coe tried his hand at developing these. The Rev. George Bush of the First Presbyterian Church in Indianapolis, however, was the acknowledged leader in this field. He had been appointed to chair a committee on questions by the State Sunday School Union in 1826. His book, *Scripture Questions*, was published the next year by the American Tract House in New York.[41] Skimming the book reveals many factual questions such as "How many are the sons of Jeptheth?" But alongside them are queries of social import such as that inserted in the study of the curse on Ham, son of Noah, "Does the prophecy excuse those who have been concerned in making slaves of Ham's posterity?"[42]

The books from the American Sunday School Union and its partners, the American Bible Society and the American Tract Society, were focused on the preeminent objectives of the Sunday schools—to increase knowledge of the Bible and to impart moral teachings. These books made up the Sunday school libraries which became decisively important in bringing literacy to the "destitute" western frontier. Some of the titles are fascinating—"Way for a Child to do Good," "Spoiled Children," "The Angels' Song," "All the World's on Stilts," "The Dying Robber," "The Conversion of John Price," "Filial Obedience," "Christian Politeness," "The Evergreen," "Sister Mary's Gloves," "Life of Peter," "The Pearl of Great Price," "Betsy Green," "The New Bonnet," "The Baby is with God," "The Sailor and His Daughter," "Temptation," "Brief Account of Mary Ann," "Cultivate a Small Field," "Little Choctaw Girl," "Emma the Dunce," "I am the Happiest," "Repentance" and "Death of a Sunday School Child."

William Levering's extensive collection of Sunday school books in the Indiana State Library contains several published before 1860. Among them are "The Old Rope Maker—The Power of Divine Grace," "The Beduoin Arabs" (Customs and Manners), "The Church and Her Enemies—Trials and Triumphs of God's People," "Confession of Faith," "My Own Story—Autobiography of a Child," "The Children's Picture Book of Good and Great Men" and "Precept on Precept"—a third series of earliest religious instruction the infant mind is capable of receiving with verses illustrative of the subject.

The purchase price on some of these was as low as 6¼¢. In the fifth year of its life, the Sunday School Union's presses on Chestnut Street in Philadelphia ran off 1,462,960 publications exclusive of 1,007,500 picture reward tickets for memorization of the Scriptures. The key to the nature of these publications is found in an 1828 report to the Annual Meeting which asserted: "No book has received the imprint but with the counsel of at least three denominations of Christians, and in no instance has a publication been ordered against a single dissenting voice. This harmony has flowed from a unity of feeling arising from the influence of common motives and the impulse of a common aim."

The elementary truths to be imparted to a child were said to be:

1. God made me.
2. Christ died for me.
3. My soul will live forever.
4. If I repent and believe in Christ, I shall be forever happy.
5. If I die in sin, I shall be forever miserable.
6. I must obey my parents and those that have the rule over me.
7. I must keep holy the Sabbath day.
8. I must read the Scriptures and learn from them what I am to believe and do.

Singing also had a high priority in the pioneer Sunday schools. The Levering Sunday School Collection includes 55 books of songs, hymns, and anthems, the oldest being *Hymns Selected and Arranged for the Sunday School of the Evangelical Lutheran Church of St. Matthew* published in Philadelphia in

1833 and Dyer's *Philadelphia Selection of Sacred Music*, 4th edition, 1828. In these books there is no more pertinent song for the Sunday school movement than "The Precious Bible"—

> What is it shows my soul the way
> To realms of everlasting day,
> And tells the danger of delay?
> It is the precious Bible.
>
> What teaches me I'm bound to love
> The glorious God who reigns above,
> And that I may His goodness prove?
> It is the precious Bible.
>
> What tells me that I soon must die
> And to the throne of judgment fly
> To meet the great Jehovah's eye?
> It is the precious Bible.

In the section "Praise and Redemption" of an 1821 hymn book of the Philadelphia Sunday and Adult School Union we find this song—

> Before Jehovah's awful throne,
> Ye nations bow, with sacred joy;
> Know that the Lord is God alone—
> He can create, and He destroy.
>
> All children are conceived in sin;
> All prove themselves impure within,
> And all each day that passes show
> How much the seeds of evil grow.
>
> Seek Jesus, He alone can give
> The grace by which a child must live;
> All other hope is false and vain;
> None enter heav'n till born again.

This was a far cry from the beloved "Jesus Wants Me for a Sunbeam to Shine for Him Each Day," which came to the fore later, or the most popular of all the Sunday school songs, "Jesus loves me this I know, for the Bible tells me so; little ones to Him belong; they are weak but He is strong."

There was also a decided preoccupation with death. An 1835 hymn book of the American Sunday School Union carried selections entitled "The Death of a Pious Child," "Death of a Scholar," "Triumph in Death," and "For a Dying Child." No. 275 was "The Fear of Death Removed," which assured the child that "Jesus can make a dying bed feel soft as down pillows are." A popular title in the Union's first 100-volume library was "A Memorial for Sunday School Boys; Being an Authentic Account of the Conversion, Experience and Happy Deaths of Twelve Sunday School Boys." These hymns and stories recognized the starkly real fact that nearly every family on the frontier had one, two, or three children who succumbed in infancy or early childhood.

Relationship to Public Education

The excellent doctoral dissertation of David M. McCord presented at Purdue University in 1976 is addressed to the question—"What relation if any existed between Sunday school and the public school in early Indiana?" The conclusion is that the Hoosier Sunday schools had an exceedingly close relationship to public education, often preceding public schools, consistently encouraging them and sustaining them when they faltered as in the loss of their tax base in the 1850's. Whether or not they knew about a clear-cut statement of Robert Raikes on such relationship, the Indiana schools in theory and practice would generally have agreed that the Sunday school may be "the instrument under God to awaken spiritual life in the poorest children and, supplemented by day classes, can form the basis of national education."[43]

A good illustration of the Sunday school as the precursor of the public school comes in a letter from John W. Parsons, who wrote from China in southern Indiana on February 20, 1833:[44]

Total abstinence from literature is generally practiced. Aside from br. Wilbur and myself there is not a literary man of any sort in the bounds. There is not a scholar in grammar or geography, or a teacher capable of instructing in them. There are some neighborhoods in which there has never been a school of any kind. Some are supplied a few months in the year with the most antiquated and unreasonable forms of teaching reading, writing, and cyphering. There is no kind of ambition for improvement and it is no more disgrace for man, woman, or child to be unable to read than to have a long nose.

At its organizing meeting in 1824, the American Sunday School Union launched a nationwide survey of Sunday schools and of public schools as well. The Union sought trustworthy information in regard to the character of common schools, method of teaching, how the school was housed, how scholars were rewarded. On the basis of the survey, the Union declared: "The meager provision which our country makes for juvenile education must be more and more enlarged until all her children may learn with equal privilege the rudiments of a common education."[45]

The Indiana Constitution drawn up in 1816 just prior to the State's admission to the Union consisted of twelve articles. The ninth provided land grants for support of schools, called for a general system of education, and established means to implement a public school fund and create public libraries. The dream envisioned in this enlightened provision, the first of its kind in a midwest constitution, was not fully realized. In 1840, according to George Dunn, State Superintendent of Common Schools, 1,521 primary and common schools were giving instruction to 48,189 children out of 273,784 between five and twenty in the state.[46] The first free public school in Indianapolis was not opened until 1853.[47] An Indiana Sunday school missionary's report in 1837 would seem to be typical of the state. He wrote:

"In 23 counties of the Wabash country there are, as we are informed, only 61 common schools, 12 select schools, and three seminaries. Several of the 23 counties have but a single school and there are five or six which have no schools at all."[48]

It was more than a coincidence that Judge John Scott, who had written the article on education in the 1816 constitution, should have been the presiding officer of the Indiana Sunday

School Union when its first annual report enunciated as policy: "Let Sabbath schools be established wherever practicable. They will answer the double purpose of paving the way for common schools, and serving as a substitute until they are generally formed. Parents and children, becoming sensible to the sweets and benefits of learning, will unite in one loud and determined call for the permanent means of education."[49] Jesse L. Holman, Sunday school pioneer, in a letter of June 8, 1830 (in the Holman Collection at Franklin College), recorded the conviction that the best teachers of public schools were also in the Sunday schools, "one school complementary to the other." Indeed, Theron Baldwin, an American Home Missionary Society spokesman, in an April 12, 1836, letter to Absalom Peters, chief executive of the Society (manuscript collection, Indiana State Library) proposed that deficiencies in the salaries of pious school teachers be paid just as were the salaries of missionaries. In 1847, the State Common School Education Convention (recommended by the Indiana General Assembly) and the State Sunday School Union were scheduled to meet in Indianapolis on the same day—May 26. Calvin Fletcher in his diary for May 25 noted: "The Sabbath and Common School Convention to attend." Among the unpublished papers of Benjamin S. Parker of Henry County collected in the State Library is this comment: "Friends' primary schools became in many respects models toward which the surrounding district schools cast their eyes, and which many of their teachers sought to rival. More than this they soon began to send their teachers into the district schools, who were gladly welcomed, and aided largely to advance the standards of education at a time when they were necessarily very low."

The Black churches were especially important in providing opportunities for the education of Negro youth. Herbert Lynn Heller in his unpublished 1951 Indiana University doctoral thesis ("Negro Education in Indiana from 1816 to 1869") states that the inevitable pattern of Negro settlement included the establishment of an African Methodist Episcopal church and an accompanying school. The Indiana Annual Conference of the AME church in 1854 appealed for "education of colored youth" and declared:

"It shall be the duty of our traveling preachers to establish and encourage day and Sabbath schools in their charges and to preach two or more sermons on the subject of education during the conference year."[50]

In 1858, an ad in the *Repository of Religion and Literature of Science and Art*, a quarterly journal put out by a group of AME ministers, announced:

"Chance for good education in Indianapolis, Ind. Send to Rev. E. Weaver, pastor AME Church in Indianapolis. Boarding can be had at fair terms. The following branches are taught: Spelling, Reading, Writing, Arithmetic, Grammar, Geography, History, Anatomy, Physiology, and Hygiene, etc. There is also a good assistant teacher in the school."[51]

The second Indiana constitution, that of 1851 which is still the State's fundamental law, provided for a system of free public schools in Indiana, but little or no funding was provided aside from that derived from the sale of the section of land in each township dedicated to education by state and federal governments. A body blow to education was struck by a State Supreme Court decision in 1854 which ruled that only state funds could be used in support of public education, including tuition, books, and teachers' salaries. Local taxes could be used for construction of buildings and the purchase of teaching apparatus.[52] The meager state funds were soon depleted. Many school terms were reduced to 2½ or 3 months. Some schools were forced to close entirely. From 1853 to 1867 there were four years in which Muncie had no schools open; the other ten years the average term was 67 days. The average salary of 3,000 teachers in Indiana in these hard years was $21.42 per month.[53] Churches were active in attacking this situation so damaging to public education. Boone's *History of Education in Indiana* reports 78 church-sponsored schools of academic grade in the 1850's. Religious leaders worked for remedial action in the legislature. The impasse was finally broken in

1867 when on March 9 the General Assembly enacted the Local School Tax Law, which gave local governments the right to levy taxes in support of education. Thereafter the public school system developed rapidly; and the involvement of the churches with general education, whether in Sunday schools or sponsored weekday schools, diminished correspondingly.

End of an Era

The decade beginning with 1860 marked the close of an era in the Indiana Sunday school movement. The time of planting schools on the Hoosier frontier was ending. With the passage of the Local School Tax law, the Sunday school rapidly declined as a major factor in general education. The primary influence of the American Sunday School Union, attuned to the pioneer period, gave place to the Sunday School Association coming as a new phenomenon in the world of the Sunday school at the end of the Civil War. Old assumptions, attitudes toward children, and style of operation were to be challenged—and largely replaced. New leaders were waiting in the wings for their day in the spotlight. In 1856, Dr. Isaac Coe ended his nineteen years of service as a vice-president of the American Sunday School Union, yielding to a younger man.

The first Indiana Sabbath School Convention held in Indianapolis October 27-29, 1857, stands as a culmination of the frontier era. The idea grew out of the Indiana Sabbath School Union which, as a uniting force in the movement, looked back to 1826. The initiator was J.W. McIntyre, head of the American Sunday School Union's field staff in Indiana. Just two years earlier, McIntyre had given a report which smacked of the frontier challenge. He and Joseph Gale in southern Indiana recorded 145 new schools organized, 99 visited and aided, 906 teachers enlisted, 6,424 new scholars enrolled, $348.60 given in libraries and textbooks, $3,355.85 worth of books sold, 11,464 miles traveled, and 251 addresses given. Reports like this had been given for thirty years as the Sunday schools were carried to the destitute places. Among those who attended the convention were Calvin Fletcher and Elijah Coffin, revered leader of the Quaker Sunday schools in the Richmond area.[54]

The object of the convention, according to the call, was to seek out the best ways of conducting and teaching Sabbath schools and to promote a more general interest in the religious education of the young and greater result from Sabbath school instruction. In a way, the convention looked back to the founding days. J.W. McIntyre was the secretary of the convention. The Rev. James Ayars of Cincinnati, district secretary of the American Sunday School Union, the keynote speaker, referred to union missionary schools. Used in the program was the child's bedtime prayer: "Now I lay me down to sleep; I pray the Lord my soul to keep." Yet, there was a look to the future in that Bishop E. R. Ames of the Methodist Episcopal Church was elected president. Of 166 schools represented by the 341 delegates, all but 23 listed denominational affiliations. The registration breakdown indicated:

Methodist Episcopal	138 from 65 schools
New and Old School Presbyterian	96 from 23 schools
Union Schools	36 from 23 schools
Baptists	18 from 14 schools
United Brethren in Christ	9 from 8 schools
Christian	12 from 8 schools
Lutheran	9 from 3 schools
Cumberland Presbyterian	2 from 2 schools
Congregationalists	4 from 2 schools
Friends	14 from 1 school
Methodist Protestant	1 from 1 school
Episcopal	1 from 1 school
Reformed Presbyterian	1 from 1 school

The Sunday school movement in Indiana had come a long way in its four decades of life. Thousands of children and adults had been drawn into its discipline of general and religious education. Public education had been stimulated and advanced. Hundreds of committed Christians had learned to work together in a common cause. Community life had been impacted positively. Lives had been changed.

On the other hand, the Hoosier Sunday schools mirrored some of the limitations of the national movement. Women, though active in the schools, were seldom accorded leadership roles. Generally, Blacks had not been integrated. No Black Sunday school was represented at the 1857 convention. Indiana seems to have gone along with the policy spelled out in the instructions of the American Sunday School Union to its missionaries and agents: "On the delicate question of slavery, abstain from all remarks; much injury may result from an indiscreet observation."

Coolness to newcomers from overseas was evidenced particularly in hostility to Roman Catholics. The August 1844 issue of *The Home Missionary,* organ of the American Home Missionary Society, featured Indiana. Among the communications was a letter from Logansport which asserted:

"The enemy is striving to possess the land. The Romanists have founded a college at South Bend and are establishing churches and schools at nearly every important point in the territory. Should the friends of a pure, spiritual Christianity be less zealous and self-denying than the votaries of a cold dead formalism?"[55]

Imperfect, yet assuredly an instrument of God for the nurture of His children, the Indiana Sunday school movement by 1860 had laid solid foundations for the advances of the post-war years.

CHAPTER II

Harvest Time

The Indiana Sunday School Union was organized in 1865 and has held a state convention every year. It achieved full county organization in 1877. In 1886-87, at least one county convention was held in every county—a total of 165. There were also a number of district conventions. Many townships are organized. One county of 12 townships held 22 township institutes, another 28. Indiana has performed all this work as a thank offering to God—never having paid a salary to any officer in its prosecution, and no county has ever been organized, or its organization perpetuated, except by an assembly of its workers called together for the purpose by advertised notice.
Report of William H. Levering, President, Indiana Sunday School Union, to the Fifth International Sunday School Convention, Chicago, June 1-3, 1887.

Great as was the era of the pioneers, the flowering of the Sunday school movement in Indiana came with the founding of the Sunday School Association. The new thrust arose under the leadership of the "Illinois Band," in which the leaders were Benjamin F. Jacobs, a Baptist layman who was a produce dealer and realtor in Chicago; a young Methodist clergyman, John H. Vincent; Edward Eggleston, a Sunday school editor

best known for his book *The Hoosier Schoolmaster*; and
William Reynolds, a Peoria businessman. The vision of the
transformation came from Dwight L. Moody and Reynolds
when in 1864 they were doing civilian religious work among
the northern troops. They determined after the war to go into
the Sunday school movement, convinced that winning children
to Christ and building them up in faith was the greatest work
in the world.[1]

At Moody's behest, Reynolds went to the Sunday school
convention in Springfield and succeeded in taking it over. The
Illinois association became the base for a revivified Sunday
school movement which swept North America and made its
impact felt around the world. The leadership was strong,
devoted, organizationally skilled. The states were soon marked
by networks of county conventions and township institutes
feeding into and guided by the state conventions. From 1875
there were international Sunday school conventions, which
included Canadian delegates and whose concerns
encompassed the world.

Within a year after the takeover of the Illinois convention by
Reynolds, Jacobs, Vincent, and the others, the Indiana Sunday
School Association had been organized, building on and
preserving the corporate name of the 40-year-old State Sunday
Union of pioneer days. The founding convention of the
Association was convened in Indianapolis on May 30, 1865, on
invitation of that city's "Friends of Sunday Schools." To it came
161 delegates from 125 schools, which reported 1,366 teachers
and 14,600 scholars.[2] The convention proclaimed as the object
of the new association "to unite all Christians throughout the
state in earnest efforts to promote the cause of Sabbath schools
and for this purpose, as far as practicable, the formation of
County and Township Sabbath School Unions throughout the
State to cooperate with this Union and this good work."

The points of discussion in that initial convention sound very
contemporary:

1. How can we secure the largest attendance of children in
our Sunday schools?

2. How can we best retain the children in our Sunday schools as they advance in years?

3. How can we secure the cooperation and attendance of parents and other adults?

4. How much time should be devoted to singing?

5. Is it desirable to engage nonprofessors of religion as officers and teachers?

6. What is the best general method of conducting a Sabbath school?

Among the resolutions of the convention was a recommendation that to secure attendance each school should elect a missionary committee to visit homes, urging parents and children to join a Sunday school. Another resolution declared that the best means to retain Sunday school enrollees was to convert them; have good libraries; good, faithful, and punctual teachers; gradation of classes; adaptation of lessons to the age groups; the presence and example of older members; the impression of moral obligations; and the teaching of the Bible as a science. Perhaps surprisingly, the convention resolved "to use unconverted persons of good moral character in the Sunday schools whenever their services can be helpful." In reference to the memorization mystique, the convention came down in favor of encouraging each child to memorize a few verses weekly rather than one or two going way out in excited contests.

Marching to Zion

The Indiana association grew rapidly. The second convention was held in New Albany June 5-7, 1866.[3] It gave a preview of Indiana conventions for the rest of the century and was typical of the assemblies of the faithful in other states. Featured was a mass meeting of all the Sunday schools in the area, which opened with a rousing rendition of the song, "The Sunday School Army." A Committee on Permanent Organization was set up and Col. John W. Ray, Indianapolis leader, was elected president. There was a lengthy discussion of the relationship of the Sunday school to the church. The outcome was a resolution which declared: "The Sabbath school is the Nursery of the Lord and it should be used as a means of replenishing the church." Another resolution called for the organization of a teachers' institute in each Congressional District.

Indications of an emerging social conscience appeared in the 1866 convention. A resolution demanded that more strenuous effort be made "to bring poor and destitute children under influence of Sabbath school instruction and culture." There was feeling that the Sunday schools were becoming a middle-class institution. On the first day, convention delegates received and tabled a resolution asking the schools to seek signers of temperance and anti-tobacco pledges. The next day a more general resolution supporting a "great temperance reformation" was adopted.

The third convention at Lafayette June 4-7, 1867, is remembered as one of the best in the first decade of the Sunday School Association. The meeting place in the opera house overflowed. A choir of 1,000 singing children charmed the convention, which also witnessed a lengthy procession of Sunday school scholars headed by the Star City Band. Leaders were pleased with the high level of enthusiasm in evidence. Hon. Will Cumback, close friend of General Lew Wallace and himself a wartime administrative leader, took over the presidency from Col. Ray, who successfully sponsored a resolution advising each school to organize a "normal class" composed of persons willing to teach, from which cadre of trained persons teachers for the classes would be selected. Other resolutions set as goals:

1. The immediate conversion of all children and their steadfastness and growth when converted.

2. Weekly teachers' meetings to prepare the teachers for their work.

3. A meeting of youth on the first Sabbath of each month.

4. A county convention annually in every county of the state.

On the organizational side, the convention recommended that

the whole school have the same lesson at the same time—a look forward to the uniform lesson idea; that the entire school repeat the opening prayer after the superintendent; and that each school organize an infant class.

The 1868 convention in Ft. Wayne marked the appearance of the comprehensive statistical report, a characteristic of all the later conventions. This first report recorded 580 schools, 46,791 scholars, an average attendance of 32,369, 2,243 scholars professing religion during the year, 80,708 volumes in libraries, 240,196 papers and pamphlets distributed, and $13,092.84 in benevolent contributions. Noteworthy on the program was the presence of Edward Eggleston, 31-year-old Sunday school publisher and soon to write *The Hoosier Schoolmaster*, among the first literary efforts dealing with day-to-day life in the West. Born at Vevay, Indiana, Eggleston used his homecoming to declare his conviction that the pulpit could not be depended upon for teaching; that full periods should be given to teachers freed from the interruption of librarians bringing round the books for loan; that time should not be "wasted on the geography of Bible lands"; that memorization was being over-emphasized; that no child "should read more than he can be taught to understand"; that conditions for rewards should be such that "they can be attained by any scholar in the school"; and that the prime objective was "to lead children to Christ."

The proceedings of the Ft. Wayne conventin played up some of the drama and color always attached to these annual gatherings. On the second day, the agenda was interrupted to hear a concert by 2,000 singing Sunday school children. In gala dress, they hurried to meeting places in their churches and chapels at 2:30 from which they marched two abreast, led by the "splendid Jones Cornet Band," to the assembly point at Wayne Street Methodist Church, largest in the city. The lively account of the day noted that with their teachers beside them, the children "fluttered along in white dresses and gay ribbons with beautiful flags and appropriate banners floating overall." Children of the host church sang "Glory Be to God"; those from

Second Presbyterian Church offered "The Volunteer Song"; from the English Lutheran Church "Land without a Storm"; and from Centenary Methodist "My House Upon a Rock." The boys and girls from the German Reformed school, singing in German, "maintained the most excellent perfect time and won a merited applause." The other selections were "Sing Jesus' Name" by the combined chorus of the Third and Fourth Presbyterian Churches; "In a Manger Laid" by the Baptist Sunday school; "Won't You Volunteer?" by the Evans Mission and Bloomingdale schools; "O Christian Awake" by the Berry Street Methodist youth; and "Shall We Gather?" by the children of First Presbyterian Church. The program closed with all present singing the Long Meter Doxology.

A Banner State

In 1873, William Levering of Lafayette, who was destined to become the inspiring and effective guiding spirit of the movement in Indiana, became for the first time an officer of the Association being appointed to collect the statewide statistics. With characteristic vigor, Levering went after his job and in 1874 was ready to report 3,116 schools with 32,643 officers and teachers and 252,000 scholars. On the strength of such a record, the Tippecanoe County leader was elected to the presidency of the Association and with "entire consecration and consummate generalship devoted time and his great physical, mental, and spiritual powers" to the full organization of the Sunday school movement in Indiana.[4] In the next three years, President Levering traveled the length and breadth of the state. He addressed hundreds of meetings, wrote over 1,000 letters, prayed, prodded, and cajoled. The result was that he could report to the 1877 convention that Indiana had achieved complete standard organization. Indiana was a "Banner State," one of only three in the nation having all of its counties organized and a county convention in every one during the year. Levering proclaimed a "Year of Jubilee" and called for thanks to God for "the thousands of children gathered in and for those who spoke His name in a whisper or with a blush but now proclaim their faith unabashed." In his presidential address, Levering asserted that these grand results had been accomplished "without the expense of one dollar to anyone connected with the association." The secret of Indiana, he declared, lay in the fact that "her sons and daughters have rendered all unto God as a thank offering for Jesus' sake." To keep things going, the President called for the choice of an Executive Board "with discrimination between emotional gas and consecrated grit."

The statistics for 1877 indicated 3,965 reporting schools, 39,357 teachers and officers, 310,936 scholars, average attendance of 217,782, 7,350 received into church membership, and $15,434.79 in benevolent contributions. Worn out with the work he had carried through so effectively, William Levering refused to accept election to a fifth term. The statewide network remained strong, bolstered by the stimulating experience which had come to many Hoosiers in the 1878 International Convention in Atlanta, where the presiding officer was Gov. Colquitt of Georgia, a veteran Sunday school teacher. Indiana was recognized as a banner state. The delegates came back filled with pride that the influential Senator Frelinghuysen of New Jersey, Congressman John Hill, and Secretary of the Navy Richard W. Thompson were Sunday school teachers. The convention in the South seemed to be a reconciling force between late enemies now comrades in the Sunday school enterprise. Three of the delegates, in visitation across Georgia after the convention, were assigned to a Black Baptist church in Chattanooga where they were thrilled with the warmth of the welcome extended to them and the spirited worship of their hosts. Before the Toronto convention of 1881, four counties had fallen asleep and Indiana had lost its standing as a banner state. In the face cf these circumstances, William Levering was persuaded to resume the presidency. He served from 1881 to 1887, and by 1884 Indiana was back on the "banner" list. In 1887, at the

International Convention in Cleveland, Indiana was not only a banner state but had the largest delegation in attendance.

The Uniform Sunday School Lessons

A highlight of this golden age of the Indiana Sunday school movement took place when the Fifth National Sunday School Convention convened at Second Presbyterian Church in Indianapolis April 16-19, 1872. It was in this convention on Hoosier soil that the Uniform or International Lesson System was established. At its convention in 1867, the Indiana Sunday School Union had adopted a resolution calling for resumption of the national conventions, which had been held in 1832, 1833, and 1859 and had then lapsed with the war. The national convention idea met with favor—not in time for a convention in 1868 but by way of a fourth national convention at Newark, New Jersey, in 1869. Col. John Ray carried to Newark a resolution from the 1867 Indiana convention advocating that the whole school have the same lesson at the same time. At Newark, Col. Ray found widespread sentiment in support of such a development. The Colonel's advocacy of the invitation from Indianapolis to hold the 1872 conclave in the Hoosier capital was heeded and the stage was set for the historic action regarding the Uniform Lessons to be taken in Indiana.[5]

The lesson proposal, championed by B.F. Jacobs of the Illinois Sunday School Convention, as representative of the superintendents section, nearly went down in the contention for adoption as the uniform lessons between two conflicting lesson series. One was that published by the *National Sunday School Teacher* edited by Edward Eggleston and the other was the Berean Series, widely used among Methodists, which had been created by the Rev. John H. Vincent, by this time head of the Sunday School Department of the Methodist Episcopal Church. B.F. Jacobs worked out a compromise resolution, which was supported by the Indiana delegation and adopted enthusiastically. The resolution read:

Resolved, That this Convention appoint a committee to consist of five clergymen and five laymen to select a course of Bible Lessons for a series of years not exceeding seven, which shall, so far as they may decide possible, embrace a general study of the whole Bible, alternating between the Old and New Testaments semiannually or quarterly, as they shall deem best, and to publish a list of such lessons as fully as possible, and at least for the two years next ensuing, as early as the first of August, 1872; and that this Convention recommend their adoption by the Sunday schools of the whole country.

Passage of this epoch-marking resolution was greeted with the triumphant singing of the Doxology. John H. Vincent became the first chairman of the International Lesson Committee serving in that capacity for twenty-four years.* Thus, the most audacious development in the history of the Sunday schools was launched—and on the soil of Indiana. Before long, one could go to a Sunday school almost anywhere in the nation and enter into the same series of Bible studies with which he was familiar at home.

Come Celebrate With Us

The Indiana Sunday school in the latter part of the Nineteenth Century was a celebrative institution. Not only did the schools avail themselves of every opportunity for celebrations in connection with anniversaries, dedications, graduations, and rally days, but they continually celebrated their call from God himself to nurture in the faith and win to life commitment the children, youth, and adults of their communities.

---

*It is interesting to note that in 1980 Indiana is contributing to the Uniform Lesson Committee through the service of Dr. F. Benjamin Davis, president of the Indiana Missionary Baptist State Convention (National Baptist of America) and pastor of New Bethel Baptist Church in Indianapolis. Dr. Davis has served on the Committee twelve years and has been its chairman from 1977 to 1980.

When the Roberts Park Methodist Episcopal Church in Indianapolis dedicated its new building in 1876,[6] the Sunday school was given a prominent place in the festivities. The officers were recognized—the superintendent, two assistant superintendents, the secretary, treasurer, and two librarians. Twenty-seven teachers were listed—thirteen men and fourteen women—plus three retired teachers, whom they called "supernumeraries," a Sunday school organist, and chorister. All the past superintendents were lifted up for honor, including Calvin Fletcher 1842-1850 and 1857-58. The "dedicating exercises" in the Sunday school itself featured responsive readings from the Psalms, such hymns as "Be Joyful in God," "The Old, Old Story," "All to Christ I Owe," and "All Hail the Power of Jesus' Name." The superintendent issued a challenge:

"Wherewithal shall a young man cleanse his ways?"

To this the school replied:

"By taking heed thereto according to His way."

Then followed a series of affirmations:

"With my whole heart have I sought Thee. O! Let me not wander from Thy commandments."

"Thy word have I hid in my heart, that I might not sin against Thee."

"Thy testimonies are my delight and my counselors."

"I have sworn it, and I will perform it, that I will keep Thy righteous judgments."

The infant class (kindergarten age apparently) had an exercise, "The Crowning of the Cross." They recited together:

This crown we bring
In honor of our Savior King,
And ask you all with us to raise
A song of triumph to His praise.

The crown upon the cross we place,
Fit emblem of redeeming grace.
The cross of Christ on earth we'll bear;
The crown bestowed by Him we'll wear.

There was a final responsive series climaxing in the declaration, "Let everything that hath breath praise the Lord. Praise ye the Lord." The Doxology and an organ postlude closed the ceremony.

One detects a changed attitude toward children in the Sunday scool of the post-war era. No longer are they little adults to be saved ere death carried them away. Rather, they are God's precious little ones, His "sunbeams" to be cherished and nurtured in the Father's way. Charles Jacobs of Indianapolis, speaking at the 1878 convention, declared, "I never expect to make a child know anything unless I have knowledge of the child himself."[7]

There was great appreciation of music—songs, anthems, solos, the Sunday school orchestra. Col. John Ray drew applause at the 1879 convention when he expressed his philosophy by quoting Charles Wesley:

"List to the notes of song.
Why should the notes be evil?
Music, alas, too long hath been
Taxed to pay the devil."

Evident, too, was more thoughtfulness for women. At the 1883 convention, the Rev. W. J. Darby of Evansville spoke to "The Mission of Woman as a Teacher of the Gospel." When he concluded, there was a motion that "the ladies rise to express their appreciation and thanks." A man requested that he and other men present be permitted to join in the testimonial so "the whole convention stood to their feet." From 1880 on, women were regularly docketed as speakers at the state convention. In 1884 Frances Willard, founder of the Woman's Christian Temperance Union, was the keynote speaker and Mrs. Mary T. Wilson of Dublin gave an address on "The Responsibilities of Parents and Teachers." Commenting on weaknesses in some county organizations revealed in the 1884 compilation of statistics, President Levering observed: "Is there a remedy? Yes, there is. Elect an earnest, consecrated woman. In all my experience in Sunday schools, I have never known a woman in an official position to neglect an undertaken duty in Christian work." An observant male delegate noted that no women had been included in the slate of nominations for the Executive Board. The report was remanded to the Nominating Committee, and two women were subsequently elected to the executive body.

The chief evidence of social concern was with respct to temperance. Having broken into the agenda at the 1866 convention, this cause maintained its place. As early as 1882, a resolution supporting prohibition for Indiana was passed. Numerous speakers on the evils of alcohol appear on convention programs. Notice was taken regularly of the work of the WCTU, and support was given to the inclusion of temperance lessons in the Uniform Series.

Denominational Sunday school concern was becoming more apparent. Notice has been taken earlier of the service of John H. Vincent as head of the national Sunday School Department of the Methodist Episcopal Church and of the Berean Lesson Series developed by Vincent and used widely among Methodists. The Disciples held their first Sunday school convention in Indianapolis in 1858. In 1868 the Indiana Christian Missionary Society was meeting jointly with the denomination's State Sunday School Association; and in 1870 the work had developed sufficiently to warrant employment of a full-time director, William W. Dowling, who was reported as giving lectures and presenting demonstration lessons.[8] In 1867 a Baptist Sunday school convention was organized. The Sunday school interest was carried at first by the resident agent of the publication society, E. A. Russell, who in 1876 reported 542 Baptist schools with 60,000 scholars. Russell was succeeded by S. H. Huffman, a layman from Seymour, who served effectively for 25 years. It is interesting to note that as late as 1885 Huffman marked the fact that only two-fifths of the Baptist churches maintained their Sunday schools year-round.[9]

Miss Anna P. Stout and Dr. Henderson S. Davis in their "History of the Sunday School Movement in Indiana—The

African Methodist Episcopal Church"[10] note that Sunday school reports were regularly included in their denomination's conference proceedings in the 1880's. At the end of the decade, 56 Sunday schools were listed with 2,187 pupils, 214 teachers, and 54 superintendents. By 1890 only one of the day schools remained which had been so much a part of the A.M.E. program in pre-Civil War days. The committee on Sunday schools pressed for teacher training and dedication. Instruction began with children on the Cradle Roll after infant baptism and "watchful care and spiritual stimulus" were provided as the students grew into adolescence. The objective was to "bring the youth to the point of meaningful commitment to Christ."

An innovation in the form of summer conference grounds appeared. In 1884 the Disciples opened Bethany Park—a 40-acre tract in Morgan County south of Indianapolis[11]—and in 1889 the Baptists launched a summer assembly program on Pine Lake near Angola north of Ft. Wayne.[12]

The classroom materials were not greatly changed from those employed in the pre-Civil War days. The chief difference was their greater uniformity and organization resulting from the adoption of the International Uniform Lessons. The Levering Collection in the State Library contains eight bound volumes of quarterlies for every age level. A typical lesson consisted of the Scripture passages for the day; the Golden Text, which would be recited by the entire school; questions on the lesson; and a final section, "What I may learn from the lesson." Included also were a glossary of terms, maps, pictures, songs, and responsive readings. And, most amazing to a present-day reader, the David C. Cook intermediate lesson quarterly covering three months of instruction sold for 2½¢ in orders of ten or more! Levering recommended as a resource for teachers *Peloubet's Selected Notes on the International Sunday School Lessons*. Another widely used help was *Tarbell's Teachers Guide*.

As he retired for the second time in 1887, William Levering seemed pleased with the situation. Speaking as president, he celebrated the large number of children won to Christ, the faithfulness of leadership. "Indiana," he affirmed, "has become conspicuous in the cause. A city set upon a hill cannot be hid." He noted that the Associated Press was covering the convention through daily stories and that railroads had given half fares to delegates. Drawing upon his voluminous correspondence, Levering cited a letter from a London Sunday school leader, who, having been documented on the Indiana methods and organizational patterns, wrote: "I confess, I find your system far more thorough than ours, and, I should say, more lasting in results as far as human agency is concerned." Levering further noted that a Hoosier visiting in Ireland marked how much the Irish Sunday school organization resembled that in Indiana. The Irish leader told him that ten years before he had attended an Indiana Sunday school convention and, impressed with what he had seen, had gone home to put the Indiana system into effect among his people. But Levering pointed to continuing needs—more commitment, better attendance, more preparation of teachers, more pleasant, attractive and cheerful schools, year-round operation, more liberal support, and *more complete statistics.*

Giants in the Land

William Levering truly stands out as a Hoosier Sunday school leader in the last half of the Nineteenth Century. His story is practically the story of the Indiana Sunday school movement after 1860.[13] William Hagy Levering was born in Ardmore, Pennsylvania, just outside Philadelphia in 1826. He began his Sunday school career at 27 months at St. Paul's Evangelical Lutheran Church. When he was eight, four women of his family's Lower Merion Baptist Church opened a "Sabbath school" in the Union School House. None of the adults could sing, so the boy became the chorister and throughout his life his voice "led the young in songs of praise." Levering arrived in Lafayette in 1851 and established there the first "one price" store in Indiana specializing in hats and furs. Later he took up real estate, a loan business, civil engineering, and insurance. He developed such expertise in insurance that he was called all over the country for consultation, especially in regard to fire losses. In this field he settled several important litigations.

Wm. H. Levering

After 1867 Levering divided his time equally between his consultation service and his vocation as Christian layman. A life-long Baptist, he was nevertheless thoroughly committed to interdenominational work, which he advocated vigorously. For 28 years he served as superintendent of the African Methodist Episcopal Sunday school in Lafayette. During this time he led two sessions each Sunday—one presenting the standard lessons, the other a "normal" school for teacher training. Active in the Indiana Sunday School Association from its founding in 1865, he served as president from 1874 to 1877 and from 1881 to 1887. In those years, 150,000 children were added to Hoosier Sunday schools, and more than 33,000 were brought into churches on confession of faith. For thirty years he was president of the Tippecanoe County Sunday School Association, which became a model with its county conventions, township institutes, and efficient organization being generally acclaimed. He was in demand as a lecturer and counselor all over Indiana and in other states as well—as many as seven in a single year. He was for many years a member of the Executive Committee of the International Sunday School Convention and attended the World Sunday School Convention in London. In all this work for "the cause," as he referred to it, Levering never accepted remuneration in any instance and defrayed his own expenses.

With a keen sense of the historical importance of his experiences, Levering preserved all his letters over 38 years, which he bound into books and indexed. He gathered state, national, and international convention proceedings, Sunday school books, song books, and quarterlies. Included were some rare records of the Black denominations with which he worked, covering the years 1873 to 1901. With two gold pens he wrote in a fine, distinct hand copious notes on his various collections and remarkable synopses of his Sunday school lessons recorded uniformly on cards. Near the end of his life in 1906 he wrote his *Historical Sketches of Sunday School Work: Sunday School Work in Indiana, North America and Beyond the Seas*. No one could have written such a book with greater authority. His career was unmatched in the annals of the Indiana Sunday school movement.

A close friend of Levering and partner in Sunday school work for many years was Col. John W. Ray of Indianapolis. At the 1879 state convention, Ray told the story of his Sunday school pilgrimage:

I remember when the spelling book and the first reader were the most used books in the Sunday school. It was no second-rate school either, for Calvin Fletcher was its superintendent and Samuel Merrill, one of the grandest men that God ever made, was my teacher. It was there I learned to love the Sunday school, and I was taught that the Bible was worth more than all other books in the world. When I left the Indianapolis school, I was given a little piece of brown paper which certified that John W. Ray had attended Sunday school. That was the only certificate of good character I had had in my life.

Col. John W. Ray

Ray attended the founding Sunday school convention of 1865 and recalled the faces of "the venerable men and godly women" who were there. He noted that at the start it was very important to give each denomination equal attention, equal time on the floor, and equal representation on committees. "But at New Albany [1866] we left all that behind and now no one is asked from what church he comes."

Ray related that the first lesson book in Indiana was *The Union Questions Book* introduced in 1836. "I remember," he recalled, "when I brought my ten cents to purchase one. From it grew the international system of topical lessons by which the children are able to grasp the points of Scripture passages as they would never have done in any other way under any other system." President of the 1867 Indiana Sunday School Convention, which resolved in favor of one lesson for all classes in the school, Ray had carried that resolution to the Fourth National Sunday School Convention at Newark in 1869 and had joined in advocating the resolution which instituted the Uniform Sunday School Lessons at the Indianapolis Convention of 1872. In regard to the Uniform Lessons, Ray declared, "The best scholars in the world have been lending their influence in the preparation of these international lessons, and today the great thought of the people of Indiana is to the best means for training the boys and girls in our Sunday schools so they may develop into the true grandeur of American manhood and womanhood." Ray gave a prophetic reference to Benjamin Harrison, of whom he said, "Go into one corner of the Sunday school room at First Presbyterian Church in Indianapolis and you will see there, with a Bible in his hand, a man being talked of for President of the United States, teaching his Bible class of young men every Sunday."

There were many other giants in the Indiana Sunday school movement. Hon. Will Cumback was one of them. President of the State Convention of 1868, Cumback was still going strong in 1892 when he welcomed the convention of that year to his hometown—Anderson. Cumback was a Civil War colonel serving as paymaster general of the Union Army. He gained fame as a writer and lecturer and was elected lieutenant governor of Indiana. In his address to the Anderson convention, this veteran protagonist shared some of his convictions about the Sunday schools:[14]

The opening and closing exercises should be of such character and conducted in such manner as to command the undivided attention of the children—conducive to perfect order in the school.... The Sunday school is exclusively a Christian institution. It is no part of the Sunday school's work to instruct in the sciences. Nor is it wise employment of time to study biographies of great men of the Bible or to learn all about the geography and topography of the Holy Land. Like Paul, the

Sunday school should know nothing but Christ and Him crucified for the sins of the world.

Hon. Will Cumback

Cumback advocated as the purpose of the Sunday school to set forth the love of God revealed in Christ. He expressed his abhorrence of the "theological wars" in some Sunday school classes and recommended that such controversies be avoided by sticking to "the word of Him who spoke with divine authority." Of the International lessons he observed: "I think the Uniform Lesson is a grand conception, but why should we wander over the time of the old dispensation when we can go at once to the New Testament and read the life of Christ and learn from His words what religion is? Let us go to the fountain at once and learn of Christ."

The leader who came closest to Levering in stature and influence was Charles D. Meigs, Jr., of Indianapolis. By profession a writer and publisher, Meigs was treasurer of the State Association for fifteen years in the late seventies and eighties and was president when the crisis of the 1891 convention was faced. He was the man, first as president and then as superintendent, who did most to pull Sunday school work out of the doldrums which came with the failure of the first employed superintendent. As superintendent beginning in 1893, Meigs originated *The Awakener*, the monthly publication of the Association, which for fifty years stood as the interpreter and promoter of the Sunday school movement in Indiana. The Home Department was one of Meigs' gifts to the movement, and he supported it vigorously. Before taking the superintendency of the Sunday School Union, Meigs had been on the staff of the Bowen-Merrill Publishing Company. In 1900 he left Indianapolis to become one of the editors of *The International Sunday School Evangel*, a monthly magazine issued from St. Louis. From St. Louis, Meigs went to Texas where he gave three years to the organization of an effective Sunday school association. When he returned to Indianapolis after eight years, Meigs immediately accepted the chairmanship of the Home Department in the State Association, which he had inaugurated during his superintendency. He founded the Meigs Publishing House, which, to the present time, is a major supplier of Sunday school materials and Christian books. When in 1918 at the age of 73 Meigs retired from his chairmanship of the Home Department, he could look back upon 41 years as a leader of the Sunday school movement.

One could mention others such as Charles Coffin of Indianapolis. In the capital city and in Kansas he gained prominence as a lawyer, but he was especially proud of his two terms as president of the State Sunday School Union and of the large men's Bible class he taught at Central Avenue Methodist Episcopal Church in Indianapolis. Another leader ws W. C. Hall, president of the Association for a decade. A traveling salesman who above all else sold the Sunday school idea, Hall held the state Sunday school program together when Superintendent John Calvin Carman left Indiana to assume the superintendency of the Colorado Sunday School Association.

Let George Do It

William Levering pointed with pride to the pure volunteer nature of the Indiana Sunday school movement. Many other presidents and members of the Executive Board gave countless hours to its operation and growth. Still there were leaders who saw a need for employed staff. They cited other states like Illinois which had moved in this direction. With Levering's departure from the presidency in 1887, the faction calling for staff leadership prevailed; and in 1888 the State Executive Committee selected the Rev. J. E. Gilbert, D.D., as the first superintendent of the state work. Dr. Gilbert had been pastor of the Meridian Street Methodist Episcopal Church in Indianapolis. He had developed a national reputation for a method of teacher training which the Indiana leaders found appealing. The memorandum of employment engaged Dr. Gilbert from November 1, 1888, to July 1, 1889, with the understanding that he would devote full time to the Indiana program. The superintendent was "to travel all over the state holding conventions, strengthening weak organizations, encouraging and assisting district and county officers and instructing teachers in the higher and advanced methods of teaching." An office was to be established in Indianapolis with secretarial assistance being made available. Dr. Gilbert's salary was set at $100 a month.

The new superintendent held that cities and towns were the strategic points for development of the state program. These leaders would be trained to go out into the surrounding countryside. Dr. Gilbert sought the support of all Christians on an *inter*-denominational, not *un*-denominational basis and persisted in recognizing and enlisting ecclesiastical bodies. All of his curricular materials were submitted for approval to a council of Indianapolis ministers of nine denominations. He set up organizations in cities with their own officers and management for the purpose of strengthening present teachers, developing "normal" (training) classes, providing lectures on religious education topics, and house-to-house visitation for enlistment of recruits. Another feature of the Gilbert system was a weekly meeting of teachers to study the upcoming Sunday school lesson.

The dream was never realized. The necessary funds did not come in. Although at the 1889 convention Dr. Gilbert reported an imposing network of 79 normal classes across the state with 3,620 enrolled, lay leadership was disturbed with decline in the county organizations reflected in a decrease of 268 in reported schools, 314 fewer officers and teachers, and a drop of 5,221 in scholar enrollment. Many felt that Dr. Gilbert had his eyes on national leadership. A national leadership development committee elected him to superintend a new branch of its work styled the Department of Instruction. The 1888 convention had voted cooperation in this enterprise and had modified the Executive Committee's memorandum of employment to permit the superintendent to work on it. An effort was made to raise funds for a headquarters in Indianapolis. This failed, and the whole idea was abandoned. Dr. Gilbert was encouraged to persevere by leaders in the West—particularly in California—and found himself often out of Indiana to counsel with them.

By 1891 it was clear that Indiana's first experiment with paid leadership had failed. Charles Meigs as president of the Association conducted for the Executive Committee a survey of the sentiment in the counties. Some of the replies to Meigs' letter of inquiry, copied in long hand by Levering into his statistical book, illustrate the problems of transition from volunteer to paid leadership. A letter from B. F. Simonson, president of the Clay County association, dated at Brazil July 22, 1891, is revealing:

Our County seemed ripe for the introduction of the methods of the State Union as prepared by the Superintendent, Dr. Gilbert. We had high hopes of that work; they have not been at all realized as yet. Our Sunday school workers are very much dissatisfied with the way Dr. Gilbert has treated us here. He has had (I am told) as many as three engagements to work in this county and has failed to appear every time. Once he was sick, but the other two times, so far as I know, he had no legitimate excuse. The dissatisfaction was increased by the fact that contributions were made with expectation that work was to be done in our county and, once at least, a contribution of about $50.00 was made from this county on the express condition that Dr. Gilbert should come and conduct an institute in this county. These hopes and promises have all failed. The result is that much dissatisfaction exists, and many schools refuse to contribute to the state work. We have many devoted and efficient teachers in our county; we need more of them. We need better trained teachers, more thorough and systematic work done, and more nineteenth century steam and electric energy infused into our work.

Other replies were of similar nature:

From Crawfordsville—Our normal class did not survive very long; have heard nothing of it for over a year.

From Whitley County—My undersanding is that the State Sunday School Union is in California and has been for some months, but hopes to reach Hoosierdom to attend the Convention in Logansport. My opinion is that we made a mistake at Rushville, and after three years' trial of new methods and the apparent failure to accomplish anything to advance the work, it would be best to take up the old system and place our state in the front rank again.

From Franklin County—Our County Association has ceased to contribute to the State Union since it became a one-man organization. Dr. Gilbert tried very hard to make us believe it was necessary to have a Normal Class, but, when we would not guarantee him one hundred dollars, it wasn't necessary at all. I am satisfied if the State Sunday School Union can be resurrected, upon the basis of years ago, Franklin County will stand by her—but under the present management we are happy by ourself.

The 1891 convention at Logansport took the inevitable step and terminated the relationship with Dr. Gilbert. William Levering wrote in the margin of the convention proceedings: "Dr. Gilbert had utterly failed in this work and left the state." The convention sought to conserve the dream by creating a Normal Training College with a Board of Regents including prominent pastors, Dr. James M. Smart, president of Purdue University; Dr. J. P. D. John, president of DePauw; Dr. Scott

Butler, president of Butler University; Dr. J. J. Mills, president of Earlham College; Dr. W. T. Stott, president of Franklin College; and such well-known laymen as G. G. Manning, superintendent of schools at Peru; Clement Studebaker, South Bend industrialist; and N. T. DePauw, a New Albany manufacturer. There is no evidence that this ambitious projection ever got off the ground. The Indiana Sunday school movement was leaderless and encumbered with a large indebtedness.

The Awakener Heralds the Twentieth Century

Sent reeling by the adversities which culminated at Logansport, the Association entered a holding operation with responsibility falling to the officers and the Rev. W. M. Bell, who was engaged as superintendent. Within a year, Bell resigned to become national missionary secretary of the United Brethren Church. Then in June, 1893, the Association turned for executive leadership to Charles D. Meigs, who as treasurer and the president elected in the 1891 crisis, had been

Charles D. Meigs, Jr.

trying to shore up the finances and organizational structure of the movement. From that point the Sunday school path led upward.

Symbol and promotional instrument of the new advance was *The Awakener*, the house organ of the Sunday school movement edited by Meigs. Volume I, Number 1, came out in October 1893. The editor described the origin of the name which he had sought to replace the rather prosaic *Indiana Sunday School Union*, the name for two years. Such appellations as "The Progress," "The Echo.," "The Journal," "The Sunday School Dynamo," "The Hot Shot," "The Elevator," and even "The Undertaker" had been suggested. Then one night, after praying for a name, Meigs awoke from sound sleep with the name "Awakener" ringing like an alarm clock in his mind. He even came up with a text for the masthead—Ephesians 5:14 "Awake thou that sleepest, and Christ shall give thee light." The publication was undertaking to:

1. Awaken a higher, deeper, and wider interest in Sunday school work.

2. Awaken more sincerity, more spirituality, more sense of responsibility in the minds and hearts of Sunday school officers and teachers.

3. Awaken hope, confidence, and encouragement in the minds and hearts of young, inexperienced teachers by impressing them with the good truth that the prayerful, conscientious efforts of a poor teacher are more acceptable to God than the third best or even second best efforts of an indifferent good teacher.

4. Awaken a feeling of guilt and shame in the hearts of some Christian people over the fact that not over 10% of the adult church members in Indiana think it worthwhile to go to Sunday school, to either study or teach the word of God.

The subscription price for the new paper was set at 25¢ per year, with agents who sold ten or more subscriptions getting 5¢ on each. Wonder of wonders, after two issues, *The Awakener* was in the black, and profits on it began to retire the debt of the

Association. As a publishing agency, *The Awakener* made a high mark. By 1897 a recapitulation of the materials coming off its presses in a twelve-month period included:

    72,000 copies of *The Awakener* itself
     9,000 printed letterheads
    15,000 printed envelopes
    53,600 canvass cards for house-to-house visitation
     3,250 home class visitors records
    14,000 home class circulars
    30,000 home class envelopes
     5,000 home class quarterly reports
     4,400 county and township constitutions
    11,000 statistical blanks
    40,767 rally day circulars and programs
   258,017 total

Meigs went after the awakening proposals of his paper with enthusiasm and intense personal dedication. By the 1896 convention at Crawfordsville he could report that he had held meetings within the year in 70 of the 92 counties. He had traveled 10,284 miles, and sent out 3,816 letters and cards, 1,836 mimeographed letters, and 1,200 printed letters. At the Crawfordsville convention, Meigs added to the usual procession of children a convention picnic at the county fairgrounds attended by 1,000 convention delegates and an estimated 4,000 from the local area. A new song providing both humor and challenge was introduced:

Where Sunday School's Only for Kids

Oh, dear, what can the matter be?
Oh, dear, what can the matter be?
Oh, dear, what can the matter be?
Where Sunday School's only for kids.

The fathers and mothers they seldom come nigh us;
Big sisters and brothers their presence deny us;
Somehow we've a feeling they're not overpious,
Where Sunday School's only for kids.

The elders and deacons don't seem much inspired;
The trustees and stewards are often "too tired";
And every last one of them ought to be fired,
Where Sunday School's only for kids.

Fruits of sincere labor were in evidence in the report to the 1898 convention, which showed in Indiana 5,617 schools—666 above Levering's banner year of 1887—enrollment of 531,442 (159,560 increase), 68,389 teachers and officers, 620 home departments, 19,234 accessions to the churches from the Sunday schools, 1,340 county and township conventions (up 101 over the previous year), and 56 banner counties having every township organized, fully officered and having at least one convention in each township. The procession that year was two miles long and required over half an hour to pass. In it were wagons carrying up to forty persons and a large contingent of horseback riders. The Association signed on the Rev. T.C. Gebauer as a fund raiser; but, unfortunately, the next year he could only report receipts to equal his salary and expenses—nothing left for the general budget. However, Gebauer was retained as part-time director of the Normal (teacher training) Department.

Indiana was in touch with national and world developments. Meigs went to the World's Sunday School Convention in London in 1898 and there spoke on "Organized Sunday School Work in America." *The Awakener* in 1899 took note of the retirement of B.F. Jacobs after nineteen years as chairman of the executive committee of the International Sunday School Convention. John Wanamaker was elected to succeed him. Such national leaders as Marion Lawrence and H.M. Hamill appeared on Indiana convention programs. The Indiana superintendent was active in the "field workers association" related to the International Convention and in 1899 was its vice-president. Furthermore, at the International Convention in Atlanta (1899), Indiana had 57 of the 231 banner counties in the nation (25%). A distant second was Missouri with 27.

Meigs offered his resignation in August 1900 to take up an editorial post with the *International Sunday School Evangel* in

St. Louis. In a little more than seven years this dynamic leader had traveled 81,366 miles, attended 469 county and township conventions, delivered 1,545 addresses, written 25,029 letters, and issued 1,471,888 pieces of printed matter. Charles Meigs was widely acclaimed for his work, which he turned over to his "beloved brother," the Rev. John Calvin Carman, who had been pastoring two small suburban Baptist churches in Indianapolis. At the 1901 convention in Shelbyville, attended by 1,500, Carman was able to report that the organization was free of debt. The popular title "Indiana Sunday School Association" was officially adopted, replacing the traditional legal title "Indiana Sunday School Union," and Miss Beulah Buchanan of Rising Sun was announced as the new managing editor of *The Awakener* and office assistant to the superintendent. Miss Buchanan thus became the first woman staff member of the Association. T.C. Gebauer was continued as the Normal Superintendent. After a successful 1902 convention, which drew 1,702 delegates to Terre Haute, Carman, faced with the breakdown of his health, resigned, accepting a call to the superintendency of the Colorado Association.

In February 1903, E. Wesley Halpenny was introduced as the new Indiana superintendent. He came from the General Secretary position in the Sunday School Union of the Province of Quebec, Canada. Stricken with typhoid fever soon after his arrival, Halpenny was unable to take up his responsibilities until fall, but he proved to be an effective workman. During his administration, the Cradle Roll appeared as a function of the Primary Department in 1904. Mrs. M.J. Baldwin was employed as superintendent of the Department on one-third time. Three new departments were added—Temperance, Missionary, and Adult Class Organization. George N. Burnie was added to staff as a field worker assisting Halpenny. And Indiana had a new state song to be carried by Hoosier delegates to the international conventions. Authored by a budding song writer, Charles M. Fillmore, and sung to the tune of "Marching Through Gerogia," the song declared:

George N. Burnie

"We're from Indiana, the good old Hoosier State.
We are always out on time though others may be late.
And we never lag behind—we're strictly up to date.
    Hip! Hip! Hurrah for Indiana!"

In 1908, C. D. Meigs returned to Indiana and took up leadership of the Home Department, which he had created. The statistics for 1908 revealed 5,210 reported schools, 64,881 teachers and officers, 475,994 total enrollment, 1,005 cradle rolls with 24,876 enrolled, 590 home departments enrolling 19,504, 1,054 conventions, 842 graduates from standard teacher training courses, and $6,716.64 in administrative expenditures.

At the end of 1909, Superintendent Halpenny resigned to return to Canada as general secretary for the Sunday school association of Ontario Province in Toronto. George N. Burnie, field worker under Halpenny, was promoted to what was now called "General Secretary." Maud Junkin Baldwin continued as children's worker and Pearl Weaver as office manager.

Professor R.A. Ogg of Kokomo, with a long career in public schools behind him, became field worker and superintendent of the Teacher Training Department on one-third time. Later in the year, when Mrs. Baldwin resigned to become elementary superintendent for the Pennsylvania Sabbath School Association, Miss Hazel Lewis became the new elementary superintendent in Indiana. The budget was $7,795. Three years later Miss Lewis resigned to take up leadership of the national department of elementary education for the Disciples.

There was much statewide interest in the Golden Jubilee State Convention, which convened at First Baptist Church in Indianapolis June 16-18, 1914. The organizational chart included in the proceedings of that convention reveals the scope of the work then being carried on. The roster of staff and department heads carried:

General Secretary—George N. Burnie

Office Secretary and Superintendent, Temperance Department—Miss Pearl L. Weaver

Superintendent, Elementary Division and Missionary Department—Miss Emma G. Lemen

Superintendent, Secondary Division, and Training Department—E. T. Albertson

Superintendent, Adult Department—A. B. Cornelius

Superintendent, Home Department—C. D. Meigs

Superintendent, Press Department—Lannes McPhetridge

Teacher education loomed as a major concern with registrations being taken for the Summer Training School at Winona Lake. Six hundred delegates from eleven states were expected for a missionary education conference at Conference Point Camp on Lake Geneva in Wisconsin. Conference Point was also offering a "School of Methods" and youth and adult camps. In 1914 the Association found a new cause—Bible courses in Indiana high schools. A resolution was adopted which declared:

"We commend every public school teacher who is practicing this privilege [of Christian witness in teaching], and we promise our encouragement to the end that in all the schools of the State the Bible, the sheet anchor of our civilization, may be heard and honored."

The 1916 Convention drew 2,239 registered delegates to Muncie and the statistics would have brought joy to the heart of William Levering. Indiana had attained a new high with 69,958 officers and teachers, 580,231 enrollment in 5,388 schools, and average attendance of 391,958. In that year the growth of the adult Bible class as a major factor in the Sunday schools was underlined by the report of 3,895 chartered adult classes placing Indiana fourth in the nation. In June 1917, 4,420 chartered adult classes were recorded. A.B. Cornelius and his colleagues in the Adult Department were hard put to keep up with the charter applications. In the decade from 1910 to 1920, the Indiana Association began holding State Older Boys and Girls Conferences, which drew hundreds of young people.

As the second decade of the century ended, Sunday school work in Indiana was reaching new heights annually. The 1919 State Convention in Muncie registered 3,000 delegates from 83 counties—the largest convention in the United States. A new structure developed in a constitutional convention on January 8, 1918, looked like this:

Children's Division—Cradle Roll, Beginners, Primary and Junior

Young People's Division—Younger Boys and Girls Department 12-14; Older Boys and Girls Department 15-17; Young Men's and Women's Department 18-24

Adult Division—Organized Bible Classes, Home Department, Parents Department

Administrative Division—Pastors, Superintendents, Secretaries, Treasurers, Home Visitation, Policy Development

Education Division—Curriculum, Temperance, Missionary, Training Department and Library Work

With George Burnie leaving to become general secretary in Illinois, E.T. Albertson moved up from superintendent of the Education Division to the position of general secretary, which he served with distinction for 23 years. Burnie had given 13 years of highly appreciated executive leadership.

The Association had moved from the Law Building to larger offices in the newly constructed Occidental Building at the corner of Illinois and Washington Streets in downtown Indianapolis, where the state Baptist and Disciples headquarters and Meigs Publishing House were also located. Sunday school leaders were proud that Governor Goodrich was one of them, teaching regularly the Business Men's Bible Class at Memorial Presbyterian Church. Indeed, it would seem that as it faced the post-war era, the Sunday school movement could declare with Robert Browning, "God's in His heaven—all's right with the world!"

CHAPTER III

Threshing Time

As a class, teachers are untrained. 87.7% of them fall below the minimum standards for public school teachers. Most teachers have had no course in the Bible, religion, or religious education at the college level and church colleges have done little toward training church school teachers.

- - - - - - - -

Lack of coordination within the denominations and of the denominations with the general movement for religious education is the most outstanding weakness revealed by the survey...Not one denomination has unified its boards into a single religious education leadership and not one has satisfactorily related itself to the general Sunday school movement. As a result, there is overwhelming evidence of friction, wastefulness, and inefficiency.

From The Indiana Survey of Religious Education of the Interchurch World Movement and the Committee on Social and Religious Surveys, 1920.

As it passed 1920, the Indiana Sunday school movement appeared to be strong and continuing to advance in numerical strength and influence. But it could not escape the challenges and controversies which were swirling around the Sunday school nationally. It is essential to examine these elements of conflict. To turn to another aspect of Hoosier folk culture, they represent threshing time. Before the coming of the combine to Indiana farms, the big threshing rigs rolled in to separate the grain from the chaff as bundle wagons picked up the shocks of wheat and oats in the fields and subjected them to the whirring blades of the separator. The Sunday school has gone through such a threshing experience.

As the twentieth century moved along, there arose in the nation a body of professional educators, college-trained and possessed of enthusiasm and drive not unlike that of the Illinois Band and of Levering and Meigs in the Hoosier Sunday school movement. They were advocates of the progressive education of John Dewey and of the child-centered school. They popularized the earlier writings of Horace Bushnell, who would rear children as though they had always been Christian, not sinful candidates for conversion. These new voices in Christian education cried out against the "gimmicks" of the Sunday school—attendance contests, ribbons and badges, the mottos, songs, picnics, processions, rally days, and Children's Day. Disagree though they frequently did among themselves, these new-style educators were united in affirming that the Sunday school must be reformed.[1] One of the leading Protestant educators of the 1920's, George H. Betts, expressed his belief that Sunday school instruction could never recover a genuine educational purpose since the traditions, the unpaid teacher force, the lack of standards, the outdated curriculum and the clergy were all against it.[2] Charles Clayton Morrison, he of the sharp pen, who edited *The Christian Century*, charged the single weekly hour led by volunteer teachers with causing a downward curve in religious literacy and respect for religion.[3]

What the new educators abhorred was illustrated by the Sunday school of 1929 in Muncie, Indiana, described in *Middletown* by Robert and Helen Lynd[4]:

A noisy earnestness characterizes the opening exercises, punctuated with much bustling to and fro by latecomers and secretaries. Hymns are sung lustily, especially the favorites with repeated choruses such as "I'm going to go to glory by and by." During the prayers of the superintendent, adults may utter frequent "Amens," while restless children stare about or idly pinch each other. The whole school listens to the reading of the lesson, after which it breaks up into little groups scattered through the room, each with an earnest teacher leaning over the back of the pew in front, facing his class—[About thirty minutes later classes are] interrupted by a bell from the platform, and the superintendent asked for "anybody wishing to leave a message"; there being no answer, the collection was announced, school papers distributed, and the school clattered out into the sunshine.

The "modern educators" centered their attack on the International Lessons, which they deemed antiquated and unsound educationally. The uniform lessons, they declared, did not recognize age differentials or the particular needs of persons at various stages of development. They championed the "graded lesson" idea and pushed the graded series, which emerged from the International Council of Religious Education after its establishment in 1922. As alternatives to the Sunday school, the progressives proposed weekday religious education on released time from the public schools; study "about religion" in the schools, especially after the Supreme Court declared against structured religious observances, Bible reading and prescribed prayers; vacation church schools; and family-centered instruction such as the Ligon character education program, which focused on families and utilized as sponsors community groups other than churches or Sunday schools.

The critics of the Sunday school advocated the name "church school" which underlined the century-long struggle between "the school of the people" and "the school of the church." The Sunday school movement historically had been interdenominational, if not un-denominational. *The Awakener* had summed it up pithily in a sharp one-liner: "Christians who will live together in heaven ought to work together on earth."[5] But in the age of conflict, denominations with programs, staff, and new curricula individually produced often appeared to stand in opposition to ecumenical Christian education.

For another thing, the Sunday schools after World War I faced an increasingly secular society. Many Americans—and Hoosiers—had no time or feeling for religious values generally or the Sunday school as the traditional transmitter of such ideals.

The Indiana Survey of Religious Education

With all these questions and conflicting forces bearing in upon them, leaders in the Indiana Sunday school movement turned to evaluation and reorganization. In Indiana there was less attention to the challenge of new methods than to the relationship with denominations and their educational programs. Hoosier leaders were aware of the emergence of the Sunday School Council of Evangelical Denominations, through which denominations nationally were coordinating their educational concerns. Since 1912 there had been unfolding before them the Indianapolis Church Federation, bringing Christians together on a broader basis than Christian education. There had even been an abortive attempt to float the "Interdenominational Council of the Churches of Indiana"—a denominationally based structure.

In the light of this background and questing, the leadership of the Indiana Sunday School Association was ready to respond when in the summer of 1919 the Interchurch World Movement proposed that religious education in Indiana be surveyed—one of five state programs regionally distributed to be so studied. Related to the Interchurch World Movement in this project were the International Sunday School Association and the Sunday School Council of Evangelical Denominations. Dr. Walter S. Athearn, professor of religious education at Boston University, was director of the survey. The survey team fielded by Dr. Athearn consisted of some thirty competent investigators. They were in the state from April 17 to June 27,

Dr. Walter S. Athearn

1920, contacting 256 churches of 33 denominations chosen to reflect a balance of agricultural and industrial settings. As the Indiana survey ended, the Interchurch World Movement suspended operation, turning over the Indiana data to the New York-based Committee on Social and Religious Surveys chaired by Dr. John R. Mott, which agreed to publish the survey findings. Hence, Massachusetts, Alabama, Kansas, and Oregon were never surveyed, and the Indiana study stands as the one comprehensive study of religious education to be produced.[6]

The findings in Indiana are carried in the first of three volumes coming out of the survey. It bears the title *The Religious Education of Protestants in an American Commonwealth.* Highlights of the survey were run off in a 40-page pamphlet—"Summary and Recommendations"—which was widely circulated in Indiana after its appearance in 1922.

The first area reported was plant, and here the survey team found buildings generally inadequate, falling short of approved national standards. The typical building rated 500 on a 1,000-point scale. Need was cited for rooms designed for religious education and community service. Heating— prevalently by hot air furnaces—was deemed inadequate, and the buildings were judged ill-protected from fire hazards.

The analysis of organization and administration revealed that, by and large, Indiana's churches had not assumed responsibility for the organizing, administering and planning of their church schools. Nine out of ten schools held their sessions for one hour prior to the worship services with only about half the time given to the classes. Youth societies— where they existed (only 46% had them)—were generally independent of the church schools. The Indiana Sunday schools clearly reflected a phenomenon of smallness. Of those

Typical Indiana Sunday School Setting

studied, 43% had fewer than 100 enrolled; 72.5% enrolled fewer than 200. In 65% the average attendance was under 100. The median school in the survey had eight teachers and five officers. The typical school had classes only—no departments, 94.7% of the rural schools being so organized, 49.3% of those in urban areas. Seventy percent of the schools were ungraded; only 2.8% were classed as "fully graded." It was found that adolescent boys and young men were practically untouched by missionary education. With respect to the raising and distributing of funds, it was found that income was derived from regular and special offerings and from individual contributions. The schools spent 55.8% of their resources on themselves and 44.2% on other religious work with denominational causes—especially missions—placing highest. The median school expended $100.75 annually and gave back $11.00 for every dollar of church investment. The median school spent nothing on salaries in education, and 72.5% of the rural schools and 43.9% of the urban schools had no expenditures for record and report forms.

The surveyors concluded that on the administrative side there was need for:

1. Organizational help for small schools.

2. Application of sound principles of educational administration.

3. Unification of the educational agencies of the local church.

4. Analysis of nonchurch agencies offering programs.

5. A uniform system of funds accounting and record keeping.

With respect to teachers and teaching, it was found that:

1. The typical teacher was a married woman of 37 with two children.

2. Teachers were recruited from children and adults with middle and later adolescents generally left out.

3. Teachers were church members joining at a median age of 14.9 with the major influences in their decisions being, in

order, home, revivals, the church school, the church service, companions and young people's meetings.

4. The average teacher had two other church responsibilities and rated punctuality and regular attendance high.

5. They believed their work to be of supreme importance and worthy of sacrifice.

With respect to schooling, 38.9% of the teachers had less than ten years of formal education, one-fourth less than 8.8 years. They said that they read from religious materials three to four hours a week including ten books per year. Few read the "progressive" religious education journals. It was found that 87.7% fell below the minimum standards for public school teachers. Most of the teachers had taken no college-level courses in Bible, religion, or religious education, and the state's church-related colleges had done little toward the training of church school teachers—one in six of their students taking a Bible course, only one in 64 a religious education course. The typical teacher had been teaching 6½ years. Teachers taught almost entirely without supervision and with little or no in-service training. Nearly all said they read the lessons carefully in advance, although most admitted that their preparation was usually Saturday night or Sunday morning. Male teachers said they worked 75.6 minutes on their lessons, women 66.7. The average superintendent was said to be 41.2 years of age, possessed of worthy motives and willing to give time to his responsibilities, though neither superintendents nor pastors generally supervised or trained their teachers. In profile, the teacher was described as a sincere, devoted Christian of mature years, untrained and unsupervised. The survey team recommended more training, regular supervision, courses in the church colleges, and efforts to recruit better-trained persons.

Turning to the denominations, the survey reported that seventeen had given information. Six of these had no formal organizaton for promotion of Sunday schools, one had only a young people's union, one a home missions organization, and one a conference secretary. Only four had religious education departments in their state boards. Eight denominations had spent nothing on Sunday schools during the five years 1915 to 1920. Seven had spent a total of $19,300 a year. In the service area, four denominations did nothing but provide literature, two provided convention speakers, two issued literature and arranged conferences, four published promotional literature, and one limited itself to correspondence. Religious education leadership was usually scattered among two or more boards, which often competed for Sunday school support. This lack of coordination was cited as a major weakness. "Not a single denomination," declared the Athearn team, "has satisfactorily related itself to the general Sunday school movement. As a result, there is overwhelming evidence of friction, wastefulness, and inefficiency. "

Of the State Association, the survey stated that it had won the enthusiastic support of Protestant churches, its conventions were the largest in history, its budget was raised by apportionments to the local schools, and allocations were paid more cheerfully than ever before. Strengths of the Association were listed as:

1. Democracy of control, membership being open broadly and the conventions functioning as true open forums.

2. Widespread interdenominational cooperation.

3. Growth through participation on the part of local workers in planning and policy making.

4. Sound principles underlying the executive and supervisory systems.

Weaknesses pointed out were:

1. Over-reliance on volunteers.

2. Inadequate staffing of the state office, and no city or county had professionally trained leadership.

The overall limitations cited included:

1. Inadequate supervision.

2. General failure of denominations to assume responsibility.

3. Inadequacy and competition within the denominational structures.

4. Failure to unify denominational and interdenominational activities.

5. Insufficient assistance to teachers and officers in localities.

Reorganization Effected

Leadership of the Indiana Sunday School Association took seriously the critique and recommendations of the Indiana Survey. A Committee of Twenty-Five on the Indiana Survey was constituted under the chairmanship of Dr. Edward R. Bartlett, who had come from superintendency of religious education in the Hennepin County Sunday School Association in Minneapolis to head the Department of Bible and Religious Education at DePauw University in Greencastle. Associated with him were such luminaries as President William Lowe Bryant of Indiana University, Bishop H.H. Fout of the United Brethren Church, Dean H. N. Sherwood of Franklin College, Dr. Frank McKibben of the new St. Joseph County Council of Religious Education, several well-respected pastors and lay workers and such denominational spokespersons as Dr. O.R. McKay, Carlos Dinsmore, Florence Carmichael, and Genefriede Harris. The Committee developed a report which highlighted major recommendations of the survey deemed most challenging to Hoosiers.[7] This report was distributed widely as a basis of discussion on the future of the Christian education enterprise in Indiana. The Committee also urged local church schools to buy Volume I of the Athearn report.

Several of the committee's members had attended the international convention in Buffalo in June 1920, which had seen the merger of the International Sunday School Association, bearer of a tradition reaching back 100 years, and the Sunday School Council of Evangelical Denominations, ten years old. The new organization was named "The Sunday School Council of Religious Education." Representation to the Council's executive committee was drawn on a 50-50 basis from territorial units in the states and Canadian provinces and from the denominations. On December 28, 1923, representatives of the Indiana denominations and of the county Sunday school organizations met at the English Hotel in Indianapolis to constitute the Indiana Sunday School Council of Religious Education. Like its national prototype, the new Indiana council had an executive committee which recognized both territorial and denominational elements. Half of this top administrative and policy-making body was to be elected by the state convention and half by the denominations affiliating.[8]

Hoosier educational leaders also proceeded to strengthen the state staff. Miss Nellie C. Young, a college-trained person with seven years' experience as a public school teacher and deep involvement in the Christian Church educational programs and in her local congregation, was elected superintendent of the Children's Division. Harry G. Rowe of Warren, Indiana, a layman of broad experience and greatly respected, was called to head the Youth Division. These additional staff persons enabled the General Secretary, E.T. Albertson, to devote more time to teacher training and servicing the county "councils," as they were now being called. For fifteen years these three constituted a team which was greatly appreciated in Indiana and acclaimed nationally.

The work in Indiana again accelerated.[9] Eighth in ranking among the states and provinces in 1920, Indiana rose to fifth in 1921 and second in 1922. The conventions of the twenties were large in attendance and well programmed. At the Indianapolis Convention of 1923 there were 4,649 registered delegates. There were 3,583 registered at Martinsville in 1927 and more than 4,000 at Logansport in 1928. In 1925 E.T. Albertson reported over 1,000 conventions, institutes, and conferences with upward of 150,000 in attendance. The General Secretary also sketched an enlarged program of vacation Bible schools and mentioned weekday religious education for the first time. In 1925 also, an ecumenical exhibit at the State Fair was inaugurated, and this presence at Indiana's great agricultural and industrial exposition has been maintained to the present time.

Top leadership was drawn as speakers and resource persons to the Indiana conventions. In 1923, Hugh Magill, General Secretary of the International Sunday School Convention of Religious Education, and Marion Lawrence, the Consulting General Secretary, addressed the convention along with Dr. Luther Weigle, Professor of Christian Nurture at Yale, and Margaret Slattery, noted writer and lecturer for young people. Drawn from Indiana were Dr. Frank McKibben, Director of Religious Education for the St. Joseph County Sunday School Council, and four denominational religious education directors. Dr. William Lowe Bryant, president of Indiana University, was elected to the presidency of the Council. In 1924, Percy R. Hayward, new International Superintendent of Young People's Work, was a well-received lecturer, as was Dr. Edward R. Bartlett, professor of Bible and Religious Education at DePauw University. In 1925, Dr. Roy Burkhart, Grace Sloan Overton, and Hayward were the keynote speakers, and Dr. H. Augustine Smith, famous director of the Boston University Singers, led the singing. On the business side, the subscription fee for *The Awakener* was raised from 25¢ to 50¢. The name of the state organization was shortened to "The Indiana Council of Religious Education."

By-Products of the Sunday Schools

Many significant movements and developments spawned by the Sunday schools exercised tremendous influence with regard to both Christian education and general education in the United States and in Indiana.

The first such notable innovation was the Chautauqua. Here, as in the case of the Sunday School Association and the International Uniform Lessons, Bishop John H. Vincent was the guiding light. Born in Alabama, but educated in the North, John Vincent became the foremost Christian educator of the Methodist Episcopal Church and one of the most influential leaders in the nation. In 1873, Vincent and Lewis Miller, an Ohio businessman and inventor, whose daughter married

Thomas Alva Edison, took over the old camp meeting grounds on Lake Chautauqua in northwestern New York. The two envisioned a national Sunday School Teachers Assembly similar to the normal schools for public school teachers of that day. They dreamed of a place where the study of the Bible and Sunday school teaching methods could be refined. The first season for the new institution was 1874. From the first it was interdenominational and nonsectarian in a Protestant sense (no Roman Catholic was included among the speakers until 1964).[10] William Rainey Harper, destined to become America's foremost adult educator, joined the Chautauqua faculty in 1883 as professor of Greek and Latin in the School of Languages. By 1894, 10,000 local study circles had been established—75% of them in towns under 3,500 population.[11] Fifty Chautauqua-style assemblies were formed, sometimes more than one in a state. Probably the six most significant were at Lakeside on Lake Erie; Winona Lake, Indiana; Boulder, Colorado; Bayview, Michigan; Franklin, Ohio; and Ocean Grove, New Jersey. In Indiana, besides the Chautauqua at Winona Lake, the Baptists inaugurated a Chautauqua near Angola on Pine Lake, one was instituted at the Assembly Grounds of the Northwest Indiana Conference of the Methodist Episcopal Church at Battle Ground, and others sprang up at several points, sometimes in tabernacles, sometimes in tents. The usual session was three to seven days. The waving of handkerchiefs, which constituted the Chautauqua salute, was marked at the Indiana Sunday School Convention of 1899. At their peak in the early 1920's, 30,000,000 Americans attended the Chautauqua offerings in 12,000 small towns and at camp grounds from coast to coast. The only one continuing today in Indiana is at Fountain Park near Remington, where an eight-day Chautauqua program is presented each August.

William Rainey Harper moved from the faculty of the Sunday-school-fostered Chautauqua in 1891 to accept the presidency of the new University of Chicago. There he developed, among other noteworthy educational offerings, an

Business Men's Bible Class-June 24, 1917 Central Avenue Methodist
Episcopal Sunday School, Indianapolis, Indiana

amazing program of adult education centered on a widespread network of correspondence courses. At one time it is said 150,000 Americans were enrolled in such courses in Hebrew and Greek. Many see the Sunday schools as the first American adult education centers and the inspiration for the adult education movement in general.[12] Harper was also the founder of the Religious Education Association, which has been a potent force for more than 75 years.

Another of the developments within the Sunday school movement was the large adult Bible classes. In December 1902, *The Awakener* drew attention to the class of 100 businessmen taught by the president of the Indiana Sunday School Association, Charles F. Coffin, at Central Avenue Methodist Episcopal Church in Indianapolis. Coffin was said to have begun his class with fourteen men nine years before. Reference to adult class organization first appeared in *The Awakener* in 1904. In August 1908, *The Awakener* reported a Bible Class Conference at Winona Lake attended by 1,000 men, who were said to have marched four abreast under the banner "The Men of North America for the Man of Galilee." Indiana had 3,895 chartered adult classes in 1916 and 4,420 in 1917. A.B. Cornelius was placed in charge of the registration of these classes for the Sunday School Association. The classes were registered into groups and charters for a Philathea, a Fidelis, or a Berean Bible class are still to be found in the archives of Indiana churches. Some of these chartered adult classes became so large that they dwarfed not only the Sunday schools from which they sprang, but the morning congregations of the sponsoring churches as well.

From about 1920, Vacation Bible Schools became a concern of the Sunday School forces. In that year, Dr. Edward R. Bartlett came from Minneapolis to the State Convention to speak to the theme "Utilizing Vacation Time for Religious Education." Soon after, the vacation schools appeared among the responsibilities of the Children's Division, and training programs were devised to prepare teachers and administrators of these summer schools of religion.

In the conventions of the early years of the Twentieth Century, resolutions began appearing in support of accredited Bible study courses in Indiana high schools. Such a program was instituted through the State Department of Public Instruction. Many Hoosier high school students in the 1920's and 1930's recorded in their accumulation of credit points toward graduation half credits for a semester study of the Old Testament or the New Testament. The classes were usually taught by pastors or religious educators outside the school faculties, and the state-administered examinations were sent to Indianapolis for grading by State Department examiners.

Indiana was the location of the pioneer American weekday religious education program. Begun in Gary in 1914 as a result of the vision of William Wirt, superintendent of that city's schools, the weekday movement spread rapidly across Indiana and over the nation.[13] Upward of 100,000 children, mostly in the fourth and fifth grades, attended released time classes at the peak of the program's popularity in Indiana. When legal decisions ruled out weekday classes within the schools themselves, the Christian education forces worked for the legalization of locally sponsored classes outside school buildings in nearby churches or mobile classrooms. The 1943 State Convention, for example, declared its support for House Bill 195, the Religious Education Bill, which allowed weekday released time classes up to 120 minutes a week.

The Sunday schools even evolved their own particular style of architecture—the famous (or to some critics, infamous) "Akron Plan." Developed in the last quarter of the nineteenth century in the Ohio city from which it took its name, the Akron-style arrangement was chosen by most all self-respecting congregations at the end of the Victorian era when they undertook construction of religious education facilities. The Akron Plan called for a theater-style central room with a stage, from which the superintendent conducted the Sunday school. This central room provided the assembly hall for opening and closing exercises and for plays, concerts and other events rising out of the Sunday school program. On the stage,

Akron Style Sunday School Facility at Central Avenue United Methodist Church, Indianapolis, Indiana

also, there was room for the Sunday school orchestra, which often played to welcome the arriving "scholars" and later marched them off to class. The assembly hall might also be the locale for the big men's Bible class, but sometimes it could only be accommodated in the sanctuary or the church dining room in the basement. The Akron design was well adapted to schools using the uniform lessons, for, from his lofty pinnacle on the stage, the superintendent could actually see into the many classes in alcoves off the central hall and sometimes off the balcony as well when such a feature was included by the architect.

Two good examples of the Akron Plan architecture in Indianapolis remaining in use are at Central Christian Church and Central Avenue United Methodist Church. The Central Avenue facility (shown in these pages) is particularly striking. The educational unit adjoins the sanctuary, but the two buildings are distinct, though both are excellent examples of the elaborate Romanesque revival style of architecture of which the Indianapolis Union Station is a third model. *The Indianapolis News* on March 25, 1900, described the educational building in detail:

> The interior of the new building is novel in appearance and convenient for Sunday school uses. The classrooms, twenty-two in number, are on the first and second floors above a full basement. Each is distinct from the others and filled with large glass doors. All the rooms are under the eye of the superintendent of the school as he watches from the rostrum. Extending in front of all the rooms on the second floor is a balcony with a brass railing.

Max R. Hyman in his *Handbook of Indianapolis* stated: "The Sunday School building of Central Avenue Methodist Church was erected in 1900 and is probably not equaled in the state for the purpose for which it was designed."

Assuredly, Akron Plan Sunday school facilities were fearful and wonderful creations, and for many years they were in vogue. From their commodious assembly halls, the songs, the prayers, the Golden Texts, the orchestra renditions, the superintendent's admonitions, and the "teached word" were wafted on high to God Himself.

Ups and Downs—Mostly Downs

As the Indiana Sunday school saga passed its seventy-fifth anniversary (1939) and looked to the fourth decade of the Twentieth Century, the winds of change were blowing once again. Solid contributions were made to "the cause" by E.T. Albertson and his team in the '30's. Jack E. Jones, an ecumenically minded Baptist minister, remembers that period with deep personal appreciation.[14] Jones recalls Dr. Reuben H. Mueller, a leader in the Evangelical Church (later bishop of the Evangelical United Brethren and, finally, of the United Methodist Church in Indiana) who served as chairman of the Youth Committee of what had been re-christened in 1934 as the Indiana Council of Christian Education. As a high school student and in college days, Jones found pleasure in driving over the state with Dr. Mueller and E.T. Albertson. Reuben Mueller's first national ecumenical office came when he was appointed from Indiana to the Board of the International Council of Religious Education. He went on to become president of the National Council of Churches and to international leadership as chairman of the World Council of Christian Education in the years immediately preceding its merger with the World Council of Churches in 1971.[15]

At the same time, there were signs of change. In 1938, Miss Nellie Young resigned from her superintendency of children's work to join the staff of Central Christian Church in Indianapolis. In September 1942, E.T. Albertson himself took leave of his office as general secretary, bowing out in favor of retirement pursuits on his 375-acre farm near Mooresville. He was succeeded by the Rev. Ralph L. Holland, who came from the pastorate of the Carrollton Avenue Evangelical and Reformed Church in Indianapolis. Within six months—at a constituting convention on January 25 and 26, 1943—the Council of Christian Education had ceased to be, having

1942

STATE CONVENTION

Indiana Council of Christian Education

Purdue University, West Lafayette

June 17, 18, 19

THEME:

"Speak to My People That They Go Forward."
—Ex. 14:15

A. W. BEAVEN

GEORGE OLIVER TAYLOR

Registration Fee

$1.00 to June 15

$1.25 After June 15

Entertainment

$1.00 Each
Single Room

75 Cents Each
Double Room

UNION BUILDING, PURDUE UNIVERSITY

Special Conferences for

CHILDREN'S WORKERS
YOUNG PEOPLE
ADULTS
SUNDAY SCHOOL OFFICERS
PASTORS
SMALL SCHOOLS
COUNTY AND TOWNSHIP WORKERS

R. H. MUELLER

J. QUINTER MILLER

For Further Information Address The Indiana Council of Christian Education, 812 Board of Trade Bldg., Indianapolis, Ind.

entered into a new life as the Division of Education in the new Indiana Council of Churches.

This kind of merger into comprehensive councils was taking place all over the country. Movement toward such unions proceeded under the impetus of the joint field staffs of the Federal Council of Churches and the International Council of Religious Eduction. They forecast the unification of these two bodies and other national ecumenical organizations in the National Council of the Churches of Christ in 1950. Dr. J. Quinter Miller of the National Council of Churches was the principal counselor to Indiana's new structure. At least two unsuccessful attempts prior to 1943 had been made to form a comprehensive cooperative organization of the churches in Indiana.[16] Proponents of the new council were the Indiana Council of Christian Education, the Indiana Council of Church Women, the Indianapolis Church Federation and the Indiana Pastors Conference, operating such 1934. The constituting convention assembled during the 1943 State Pastors Conference. Bishop Fred L. Dennis of the United Brethren in Christ was elected president. The declared purpose was "to promote the spirit of oneness among the churches of Indiana and to furnish an interdenominational agency for cooperation in all practical fields of Christian life and work in advancing the cause of Jesus Christ and the Kingdom of God." An *Awakener* editorial hailed the "new day in Indiana work" and expressed eagerness "to go a step further and begin to advance the cause of Christian education as part of a more comprehensive statewide agency."[17] Soon after, *The Awakener* was discontinued to become *The Indiana Church Councilor*, house organ of the new council of churches.

The newly founded organization set out on a rough road. Dr. Holland, the new executive secretary, who began his work with a deficit of $1,500, has written[18]: "It was an uphill struggle at first. There had to be an educational program carried on among the denominations of the state aimed at working together in areas other than Christian education alone. Funds were slow to come in. In fact, I had to borrow on my life insurance policy to keep our family going for a while. Gradually, however, as the ecumenical idea took hold, denominations began to contribute to the Council and its real work could then begin." In reality, the Council during Dr. Holland's period of service was never wholly free of financial problems. Through a foundation grant, an associate executive secretary, the Rev. Arthur Anderson, was employed to spearhead the Christian education work. With the expiration of the grant, it was necessary to discontinue the associate position since denominational funding had not risen to the point that it could be sustained. Dr. Holland had to carry on alone, aided by a committed corps of lay volunteers. County councils were nurtured, their conventions, institutes, and training schools were serviced, and a statewide system of training for vacation church school teachers and administrators was instituted. But denominational programming in Christian education and youth ministry was on the up-swing. Their own curricula and training procedures tended to take over from the ecumenical agency. Finally, faced with dwindling interest and declining attendance, the Council wrote "Finis" to the State Sunday School Convention, which for over 85 years had assembled annually faithful disciples of Christian education. After the demise of the State Convention, the county organizations fell away one by one so that by the middle '50's barely half a dozen remained.

In 1955, after twelve years of service, Dr. Holland resigned to become executive secretary of the Greater Worcester (Massachusetts) Council of Churches. Still plagued financially, the Council in the next year passed through a testing time when the whole ecumenical enterprise hung in the balance. Denominational executives assumed responsibility for various phases of the program led by Dr. Roy Mueller of the Presbyterian synod, the president. It was in this time of crisis that Mrs. Lillian R. King came to the staff beginning a career of 23 years characterized by steadfast and efficient service. By the end of the year the leaders of the churches had determined to move forward and Dr. Walter Hand, a Baptist minister from Indianapolis, was called as the second executive secretary. Dr. Hand served only three years before returning to the parish ministry, but he built solid relationships with the denominations and broadened financial support by supplementing denominational giving with individual and corporation gifts.

In 1959, Dr. Hand was succeeded by Dr. Grover L. Hartman, who came from the executive secretaryship of the Council of Churches of St. Joseph County at South Bend. Already a veteran of seventeen years in council administration, Dr. Hartman determined to strengthen and expand the service program of the Council. Christian education was the first area to be addressed, and in 1960 the Rev. Chauncey J. Varner was called from the Pennsylvania Council of Churches and Sabbath School Association to become associate executive secretary for Christian education. Varner renewed and strengthened all of the training programs of the Council and launched the Ecumenical Youth Encounter, which restored something of the ecumenical spirit characteristic of the State Boys and Girls Conferences of the previous generation. He also brought to Indiana the Bauman Bible Telecourse, which for fifteen years enrolled hundreds of students in a high-quality program of Bible study. Through the early years of this program many of the participants in the course came to Indianapolis for term examinations leading to college credit offered by DePauw University.

After six years Mr. Varner returned to Pennsylvania. He was succeeded by the Rev. Walter F. Horlander, well grounded in the Christian education programs of the United Church of Christ and the National Council of Churches. He has continued as associate executive director with responsibility for Christian education since 1966. Thus in the '60's and '70's when portfolios in Christian education were disappearing rapidly from the rosters of state and metropolitan councils concentrating on missional concerns and urban ministries, the Indiana Council of Churches maintained its staff leadership and kept at the educational ministry to which it had been committed at its creation.

Walter Horlander has summed up Indiana's Christian education experience in the past twenty years[19]:

In the late 1950's and early 1960's Christian education concerns were receiving high priority in Indiana both denominationally and ecumenically. The Indiana and Ohio Councils of Churches sponsored annually a seminar for training leadership for summer camping programs. The Ecumenical Youth Encounter brought youth together across denominational lines for a week-long camping experience. This was hailed as the annual event for the education of young people in ecumenism. Indiana continued to offer strong programs of weekday religious education. The thirty or more systems across the state involved upwards of 75,000 children, mostly fourth and fifth graders, in programs on released time from the public schools. Local leaders were formed into a Weekday Teachers' Association, which met regularly for in-service training and exchange of ideas. Teams provided by the Council criss-crossed the state for cooperative vacation church school workshops.

On the adult education scene, the Bauman Bible Telecourse was sponsored by the Indiana Council of Churches along with DePauw University and WFBM-TV (Channel 6) in Indianapolis. For fifteen years, the telecourse maintained the highest rating in religious programming in central Indiana, and it was also aired in Ft. Wayne, South Bend, and Evansville. Because of the strength of the program in Indiana, the producers of the telecourse in Washington, D.C., opened an Indianapolis office to facilitate distribution of the films and materials. Indiana also entered wholeheartedly into literacy education using the "Each One Teach One" approach of Dr. Frank Laubach. Beginning with illiterate migrant farm workers, the program expanded with nearly 1,000 tutors across the state serving functionally illiterate adults wherever they appeared. The Council provided part-time staff to forward this educational ministry.

New curricular resources in the denominations began to produce new materials. The National Council of Churches through cooperative publishers came out with a new curriculum for use in weekday religious education. This Through-the-Week material was designed to focus the Christian faith on four areas of the public school learning process—science, history, society, and the self. The high priority accorded Christian education among the denominations was reflected in the number of professionals working not only in judicatory offices but in local churches as directors of Christian education. The priority and specialization were also evident in the structure of the State Council's Division of Christian Education, which was divided according to age groups into departments concerned with children, youth, and adults.

By the late '60's and early '70's, the scene changed. Denominational staffs were reduced. Where there had been multiple staffs in Christian education, now there was one or none. Where a staff position was maintained, assignments were made beyond the Christian education concern. The Ecumenical Youth Encounter was phased out as were the Council's age group departments. These developments led to a redefining of the Council's Division of Christian Education, which became the Division of Educational Ministries, reflecting the view of the churches that the Christian nurture function was to penetrate in an inclusive way the total life of the church. The reasons for this shift in denominational strategy were no doubt many, but certainly the financial crunch beginning to be felt was at the center. Also, the churches were faced with a new challenge arising from the urban crisis. The needs and rights of the poor and disenfranchised came to the top of the churches' agenda. The retrenchment and reordering of priorities produced a new denominationalism, which in turn took its toll on ecumenical structures and programs.

In the past few years, the Sunday schools of the Council's member denominations have generally presented a picture of decline.[20] As an example, average attendance in Sunday schools of the Indiana Baptist Convention (American Baptist) fell from 48,928 in 1958 to 34,375 in 1975 (a 30% drop). Compilation of figures from the antecedent judicatories of the Evangelical United Brethren and Methodist Conferences has made possible a comparison with current Sunday school statistics. Here is the story for the past eighteen years:

Year	Sunday School Enrollment	Average Attendance
1960	335,033	169,562
1975	198,370	100,002
1978	183,656	90,349

This drastic decline amounts to 45% in total enrollment and 47% in average attendance. This trend is common to the mainline ecumenical churches in Indiana. Dr. Henderson S. Davis, in analyzing the experience of the African Methodist Episcopal Church, notes that young people no longer needing the church's day school or Sunday school to secure educational opportunities turned aside from both church and Sunday school. "The decline reported over the last ten years in other communions has shown up among us."

On the other hand, the Southern Baptist Sunday school in Indiana has been a growing institution. From 1946, when the Southern Baptists had only nine churches in the state, to 1959, when their state convention was constituted with 119 churches in relationship, Sunday school enrollment grew from 655 to 25,226. In 1970, the Sunday school enrollment in the churches related to the convention—by then 226 in number—had climbed to 41,787, an increase of 65%. No longer are the big Sunday schools in Indiana Methodist, American Baptist, Disciple, or Presbyterian. They are among the Southern Baptists, the Assemblies of God, and the independent fundamental Baptists and Christians. First Baptist church in Hammond (which left the Indiana Baptist Convention, once its sponsor as a mission) and the Indianapolis Baptist Temple contend for recognition as the sites of the largest Sunday schools in Indiana, both claiming more than 5,000 enrollees. Fleets of buses fan out from churches of this kind, gathering in the children not being reached by the mainline churches. These churches are reviving the Indiana Sunday school convention and in their organization and operation utilize many of the patterns and "gimmicks" of the Sunday schools of 1900. One wonders whether this situation represents the old-time Sunday school winning out over the modern church school. Certainly the fundamental churches are quick to assert that they now carry the Sunday school banner in the religious education procession and that the more liberal churches are left behind questing for the path of tomorrow.

Epilogue

I would not particularly want to go back to the opening exercises and gimmickry of the Sunday school of my boyhood, but somehow we have got to recapture the enthusiasm and spirit of its leaders.

Observation of an Indiana pastor.

We have lost the passions and convictions of our historic calling. As a result, it is not unreasonable that we should have gut-wrenching questions about who we are and whether or not what we are about is our appropriate business.

Dr. John H. Westerhoff at the 75th anniversary celebration of the Religious Education Association, November 21, 1978.

In the opening lines of Dante's "Inferno" are these highly descriptive words: "In the middle of the journey of our life, I came to my senses in a dark forest for I had lost the straight path."[1] Christian education today is experiencing a similar awakening. Somehow the path has been lost. The children, youth, and adults of the churches and of our communities are not being reached as completely as in the past with Christian nurture and the challenge to commitment of life. Many of us were reared in the Sunday school of yesterday. It effected our confessions of the Christ and summoned us to lives of service within the churches and their environing communities. The Sunday school has declined in our denominations. This is no time for lamentation over the situation or to demand re-establishment of the Sunday school as it was fifty years ago. But it is timely to inquire, "What have we now to serve as the nursery of the church, preparing tender plants for growth in the garden of the Lord of life? Have we something new to offer or can we reclaim the Sunday school as the church's instrument for renewal and evangelism?"

In the Southern Baptist Church, Sunday schools are growing. With this Christian group there is no separation between education and evangelism.[2] Is it possible with a Southern Baptist Sunday school teacher in the White House that the time is at hand for the revivification of the church school? We have drifted a long way in leadership of both church and state from the declaration of President William Howard Taft to the sixth World's Sunday School Convention held in Washington, D.C., in 1910. Mr. Taft asserted: "No matter what views are taken of general education, we all agree—Protestant, Catholic, and Jew alike—that Sunday-school education is absolutely necessary to secure moral uplift and religious spirit."[3] Has the time not come for a clarification of national and personal values and for bringing into being a "school for God's people" as relevant and effective as the Sunday school was for the generation now growing old?

Within the churches and their educational leadership there are heartening signs of willingness to grapple with the overpowering issues of nurture and commitment. In Indiana, the African Methodist Episcopal Church has since 1977 centered its programming efforts on broader youth involvement. At the annual Sunday school convention each of the last three years there has been a "Bible Bowl" and planned mass evangelism.[4] The results have been increased enthusiasm and more than twenty conversions in each convention. United Methodists of the South Indiana Conference have laid out a two-year plan involving goals for recruitment and training of teachers, promotion of the church school and increasing the scope and effectiveness of the nurturing process.[5]

The Indiana Council of Churches has covenanted to place concentrated and committed futuring at the heart of its observance of the 200th anniversary of the Gloucester Sunday school. The process began with the annual faith and order conference in November where national and state leaders shared their vision of theological foundations for education and for ecumenism. It was continued in the 1980 Indiana Pastors Conference which focused on education. This book is a part of the process as it provides a look back to roots and past successes as a means to encourage a look to the future and acceptance of its challenges and opportunities. The observance will climax in a statewide colloquy on the Future of Christian Education in the fall, assembling educators to confront together the imperatives of church-centered education in the third century of the Sunday school. A start in this direction was made in 1972 when Roman Catholics and Jews joined Protestants in an exploratory and evaluative Indiana Ecumenical Teaching Ministry Conference.

To speak personally, I am convinced that Christian education is essential to the continuation of the Church. From this source has come the bulk of church membership and through it Christians have been disciplined and nourished spiritually.

It is told that in his old age Robert Raikes stood again where he had begun and said: "On this spot I stood when I saw the destitution of the children and the desecration of the Sabbath by the inhabitants of the town; and I asked, 'Can nothing be done?' and a voice answered, 'Try'; and I did try and see what God hath wrought."[7] Perhaps, if at this juncture in the history of Christ's Church we face honestly the challenge of the hour and try to do what we determine to do, we, too, sometime ahead can look back upon our efforts and say, "See what God hath wrought."

Notes

Prologue

1. Robert W. Lynn and Elliott Wright, *The Big Little School* (New York: Harper and Row, 1971) pp. 4 and 5; Gerald E. Knoff, "Robert Raikes, You Can Try." *The Church School*, October, 1979.
2. G. Webster, *Memoir of Robert Raikes* (Nottingham: G.W. Webster, 1873) p. 15.
3. Joseph Ivimey, *Memoir of William Fox, Esq.* (London: Printed for George Wightman, 1831) p. 18.
4. Lynn and Wright, *op. cit.*, pp. 3 and 4.
5. "The Sunday School Comes South: The First Hundred Years," *Historical Foundation News* (Presbyterian Church U.S.) November, 1979, p. 2.
6. Donald A. Courtney, "Unusual Bits of Information," Board of Christian Education, Church of God (Anderson, Indiana) 1979.
7. D. Campbell Wyckoff, "As American as Crab Grass: The Protestant Sunday School," *Religious Education*, January-February, 1980, p. 27.
8. Lynn and Wright, *op. cit.*, pp. 18 and 19.
9. The American Sunday School Union, "Sixth Annual Report," Philadelphia, May, 1830.

Chapter I

1. W. H. Levering, *Historical Sketches of Sunday School Work: Sunday School Work in Indiana, North America and Beyond the Seas* (Indianapolis: The Awakener Press, 1906) p. 8.
2. Isaac Reed, *The Christian Traveller in Five Parts including Nine Years and Eighteen Thousand Miles* (New York: J. and J. Harper, 1828) p. 89.
3. Levering, *op. cit.*, p. 6.
4. Logan Esary, *History of Indiana from Its Exploration to 1922* (Dayton, Ohio: Dayton Historical Publishing Company, 1923) and William E. Wilson, *Indiana—A History* (Bloomington: Indiana University Press, 1966).
5. Grover L. Hartman, "Brookston: The Cultural Evolution of An Indiana Agricultural Community 1829 to 1940" (Doctoral

Dissertation, The American University, Washington, D.C. 1946) p. 9.

6. Richard L. Power, "Wet Lands and the Hoosier Stereotype," *Mississippi Valley Historical Review*, Vol. XXII (June, 1935) p. 34.

7. Horace Greeley, *Recollections of a Busy Life* (New York: J. B. Ford and Company, 1868) pp. 560-68.

8. Adam B. Condo, *History of the Indiana Conference of the Church of the United Brethren in Christ* (published by the Conference, 1926) pp. 15-17.

9. *Fifteenth Annual Session of the Indiana Sunday School Association* (Chicago: F.H. Revell, 1879) pp. 5-7.

10. James Albert Woodburn, "Pioneer Presbyterians in Indiana," an address at the Centennial Meeting of the Indiana Synod, Vincennes, 1926, p. 3; Isaac Reed, *op. cit.*, pp. 86-88.

11. "One Hundredth Anniversary of the Union Sabbath School in Indianapolis, April 6, 1823, to April 1, 1923," in Manuscript Division, Indiana State Library.

12. John F. Cady, *The Baptist Church in Indiana* (Berne, Indiana: The Berne Witness Co., 1942) p. 96.

13. Jesse Holman comes to life in the 150 letters which compose the Holman Collection in the Franklin College library; valuable also is I. George Blake, *The Holmans of Veraestau* (Oxford, Ohio: Mississippi Valley Press, 1943) *passim*.

14. Cited in reprint of Annual Report, Davies County Sunday School Union, July 5, 1829, to September 1, 1830, in Washington, Indiana, *Evening Gazette*, February 9, 1883; Centennial Memorial, First Presbyterian Church, Indianapolis (Greenfield: William Mitchell and Co., 1925).

15. T.H. Ball, *The Sunday Schools of Lake County* (Crown Point: The Lake County Sunday School Association, 1891).

16. Reed, *op. cit.*, p. 34.

17. *Ibid.*, p. 7.

18. *Indiana Letters: Abstracts of Letters from Missionaries on the Indiana Frontier to the American Home Missionary Society*, edited by L.C. Rudolph, W.W. Wimberly, Thomas W. Clayton with the collaboration of Jane L. Conger (Bloomington: Indiana University, 1978)—Abstract 1072, April 1, 1842.

19. Peter Cartwright, *Autobiography* (New York: Abingdon Press, 1956) p. 136.

20. *Centennial First Church Indianapolis*, cited above, p. 214.

21. Reed, *op. cit.*, p. 71.

22. Milo F. Kauffmann, *The Rise and Development of Sunday Schools in the Mennonite Church in Indiana* (an unpublished master's thesis in religious education at the Presbyterian Theological Seminary, Chicago, 1931) p. 12.

23. Robert W. Steffer, "Bobby Wild Goose and His Ragged Regiment," *The Disciple*, February 17, 1980, pp. 14 and 15.

24. Henry K. Shaw, *Hoosier Disciples* (St. Louis: Bethany Press, 1966) p. 181.

25. Martin A. Haendschke, *The Sunday School Story—The History of the Sunday School in the Lutheran Church (Missouri Synod)* (River Forest, Illinois: Lutheran Education Association, 1963) *passim.*

26. Robert Emory, *History of the Discipline of the Methodist Episcopal Church* (New York: C. Lane and P.P. Sandford, 1844) p. 147.

27. The story is told in a letter dated November 10, 1834, sent by M. Jennings, secretary of the Greencastle school, to James Ray and inserted by Ray in the Minutes of the Fourth Annual Meeting of the Indiana Sunday School Union in 1868.

28. *Herald of Truth*, January, 1867, p. 11. In addition to files of the *Herald of Truth* the Mennonite Historical Library at Goshen College has all of the Indiana-Michigan Conference reports including reports of the Christian Workers Conferences.

29. Quoted in L.C. Rudolph, *Hoosier Zion* (New Haven: Yale University Press, 1963) pp. 52 and 53.

30. *Centennial Memorial, supra cit.*, p. 213.

31. *Ibid.*, pp. 213-14.

32. *Ibid.*, p. 218.

33. *The Diary of Calvin Fletcher* in six volumes edited by Gayle Thornbrough and Dorothy Riker (Indianapolis: Indiana State Historical Society, 1972) *passim.*

34. Harry J. Sievers, S.J., *Life of Benjamin Harrison*, 3 volumes (Chicago: Henry Regnery Co., 1952) Vol. II, p. 113 ff.

35. *Centennial Memorial, supra cit.*, p. 141.

36. *Indianapolis Journal*, July 1, 1888, in *Benjamin Harrison Scrapbook*, No. 6, p. 6 (manuscript collection).

37. Lynn and Wright, *op. cit.*, p. 71.

38. Jane M. Ketcham, "History of Second Presbyterian Church during the Incumbency of Henry Ward Beecher" (Manuscript in Indiana State Library) pp. 4 and 5.

39. William Tallack, *Friendly Sketches in America* (London: A.W. Bennett, 1861) pp. 233-37.

40. "First Annual Report of the American Sunday School Union," May 24, 1825 (Philadelphia: I. Ashmead and Co., 1825).

41. George Bush, *Scripture Questions Designed Principally for Adult Bible Classes* (New York: American Tract Society House, 1827).

42. *Ibid.*, p. 26.

43. J. Henry Harris, *The Story of Robert Raikes for the Young* (Philadelphia: The American Sunday School Union, 1900) p. 47.

44. Calvin B. Goodykoontz, *Home Missions on the American Frontier* (Caldwell, Idaho: Caxton Printers, 1939) p. 217.

45. Cited in McCord dissertation on relation of Sunday school and public school, Purdue University, 1976.

46. A State Document (Indianapolis: Dowling and Cole, State Printers, 1844) p. 327.

47. Charles W. Moore, *Caleb Mills and the Indiana School System* (Indianapolis: Wood-Weaver Printing Co., 1905) p. 363.

48. Thirteenth Annual Report of the American Sunday School Union, Philadelphia, May 23, 1837.

49. Rudolph, *op. cit.*, p. 165.

50. "Journal of the Proceedings of the Fifteenth Annual Conference of the African Methodist Episcopal Church for the District of Indiana 1854," pp. 16 and 17.

51. Heller thesis, p. 170.

52. Richard G. Boone, *A History of Education in Indiana* (New York: D. Appleton and Co., 1892) p. 155.

53. *Ibid.*, pp. 155 ff.

54. *Journal of the First Sabbath School Convention* (Indianapolis: Cameron and McNeely, 1858) given to William Levering by the family of Elijah Coffin in 1903.

55. *The Home Missionary*, published by the Executive Committee of the American Home Missionary Society, New York, August 1844, p. 74.

Chapter II

1. Lynn and Wright, *op. cit.*, pp. 55 and 56.
2. *Proceedings of the 1865 Convention*, First Baptist Church, Indianapolis, May 30, 31 and June 1.
3. The report of this convention and the highlights of those which followed were gleaned from the general collection in the State Library and from the collection in the manuscript section of the State Historical Society Library presented by Mrs. Bessie Williams, long-time administrative secretary in the office of the Indiana Council of Religious Education.
4. *32nd General Convention, Ohio Sunday School Association,* Marietta, Ohio, June 2-4, 1891 (Sunday School Centennial in Ohio)—Address on "Sunday Schools in Indiana" by Timothy Michelson of Richmond, pp. 171 ff.
5. The story of this historic convention is detailed in *Centennial Celebration: Our Heritage in Uniform Lessons 1872-1972* (St. Louis: Bethany Press, 1972). The centennial celebration, appropriately, was conducted at Second Presbyterian Church in Indianapolis, that church having been the location of the 1872 convention.
6. Roberts Park "Dedication" and "Sunday School Exercises" are among the archives of churches being systematically assembled in the manuscript collection of the State Historical Society Library.
7. *Fourteenth Annual Session, Indiana Sunday School Association,* Indianapolis June 25-27, 1878, p. 26.
8. Shaw, *op. cit.*, pp. 181-204.
9. Cady, *op. cit.*, pp. 219 and 220.
10. Prepared for this history of the Indiana Sunday schools by Miss Stout and Dr. Davis in March, 1980, and presented to the author in manuscript form.
11. Shaw, *op. cit.*, pp. 239-240.
12. Cady, *op. cit.*, p. 221.
13. "William Hagy Levering" in Col. John Levering, *Levering Family History and Genealogy* (Indianapolis: Wm. B. Burford, 1897) issued by the Levering Historical Association, pp. 891-93.
14. *Lectures and Addresses by Will Cumback*—with an introduction by John Clark Ridpath, L.L.D. (Cincinnati: Craston and Curts, 1892) pp. 427-439.

15. *Twenty-fourth Annual Session, Indiana Sunday School Association 1, Methodist Episcopal Church, Rushville, June 19-21, 1888.*

16. A practically complete set of *The Awakener* from 1893 to 1942 is to be found at the Indiana State Library. *The Indiana Church Councilor*, published by the Indiana Council of Churches, continues *The Awakener* in its numbering. The March 1980 issue of *The Councilor* is Vol. 88, No. 1.

17. Report to the Thirty-Third Annual Convention, Winona Assembly Grounds, Warsaw, Indiana, June 15-17, 1897.

Chapter III

1. This conflict in the Twentieth Century religious education is described briefly but effectively in Lynn and Wright, *The Big Little School, supra cit.*, chapter v.

2. "If the Sunday School Fails," *The Christian Century*, (XLII, January 29, 1925) p. 155.

3. "Protestantism and the Public School," *The Christian Century*, (LXIII, April 17, 1946) p. 490.

4. Robert and Helen S. Lynd, *Middletown* (New York: Harcourt, Brace and Co., 1929) pp. 388-89.

5. *The Awakener*, August, 1918.

6. In addition to the summary volume entitled *The Religious Education of Protestants in an American Commonwealth* published in new York in 1923 by the George H. Doran Company, the other volumes were *Measurements and Standards in Religious Education* and *Religious Education Survey Schedules*, both published by Doran in 1924.

7. The Committee's report carrying the names and locations of the twenty-five members is preserved in the historical files of the Indiana Council of Churches.

8. This meeting was reported in the January, 1924, issue of *The Awakener*.

9. The review of the decade of the 1920's comes from the pages of *The Awakener* and the Annual Convention Reports carried in this state paper.

10. *The Christian*, July 15, 1973.

11. C. Hartley Grattan, *In Quest of Knowledge* (New York: Association Press, 1955), *passim*.

12. Grattan, *ibid.*
13. Erwin R. Shaver, *The Weekday Church School* (Boston: The Pilgrim Press, 1956) p. 13.
14. Letter of the Rev. Jack E. Jones to Grover Hartman on the occasion of the Centennial of the Indiana Sunday School Association, January 17, 1964.
15. For the story of Bishop Mueller and the W.C.C.E. see Gerald E. Knoff, *The World Sunday School Movement* (New York: The Seabury Press, 1979).
16. "Retrospect and Prospect: The Indiana Council of Churches at Age Thirty-Five," a paper prepared by Dr. Grover L. Hartman in January 1978.
17. *The Awakener*, January, 1943.
18. From an historical sketch prepared by Dr. Holland, now living in Austin, Texas, for the Thirty-Fifth Anniversary of the Council, January 1978.
19. Walter F. Horlander, "Memorandum on Christian Education in Indiana," April, 1980.
20. Appreciation is due to staff of the Indiana Baptist Convention (American Baptist), the State Convention of Baptists in Indiana (Southern Baptist) and the South Indiana Conference of the United Methodist Church for gathering relevant statistics.

Epilogue

1. Cited in John H. Westerhoff's address "Calling Forth the Future" reproduced in *Religious Education*, Vol. 75, No. 1, January-February 1980. p. 56.
2. G. Temp Sparkman, "The Southern Baptist Sunday School Today," *Religious Education*, January-February 1980. pp. 18, 19.
3. Lynn and Wright, *op. cit.*, p. 76.
4. Stout and Davis, *op. cit.*, p. 3.
5. Provided by Division on Education, South Indiana Conference, The United Methodist Church, April 1980.
6. The addresses at the Indiana faith and order conference are carried in *Mid-Stream*, Vol. XIX, No. 1, January 1980.
7. Ohio Sunday School Association, *First Centennial Celebration, 1791-1891*, pp. 177 and 178.

Thirty=Fifth Annual Convention

......OF THE......

Tippecanoe County

Sunday School Union,

TO BE HELD ON

FRIDAY, JANUARY 25, 1901.

At the First Presbyterian Church, (Sixth and Columbia Sts.) LaFayette.

Program.

9:30   Devotional Service, led by   -   -   Dr. John P. Hale

10:00   Reading of Minutes

10:10   "The Religious Life of Boys,"
       Phil Bevis, General Secretary Y. M. C. A.

10:30   Discussion, led by   -   -   -   -   Mrs. Ralph D. Moore

11:00   "The Greatest Needs of the Sunday School and
       How They Can be Met,"   Miss Addie Borum, Odell, Ind.

11:20   Discussion, led by   -   -   .   -   Mrs. F. N. Palmer

11:40   Report of Vice-President First District.
       Appointment of Committees.
       Miscellaneous Business.

12:00   Adjournment.

......DINNER......

1:30   Song Service, conducted by   -   -   Prof. J. S. Bergen

2:00   "Progress of Nineteenth Century,"   -   Wm. H. Levering

2:20   Discussion, led by,   -   -   -   -   Asa B Wasson

2:40   "Discipline of Teachers,"   -   -   -   Rev. G. W. Infield

3:00   Discussion, led by   -   -   -   Rev J. D. Coverstone

3:20   "The Church Members' Responsibility,"   Rev. A. G. Detch

3:40   Discussion, led by   -   -   -   -   Dr. J. W. Yager
       Election of Officers.
       Adjournment.

The Singing will be conducted by Prof. J. S. Bergen.

Mrs. Fannie O. Boggs,   Wm. H. Levering,
     Secretary.   President.

EVERYBODY COME.

PLEASE READ THIS BEFORE YOUR S. S. AND CHURCH.

MORNING JOURNAL PRINT.

INDIANA.

REPORT TO THE FIFTH INTERNATIONAL (TENTH NATIONAL) SUNDAY
SCHOOL CONVENTION,

HELD IN THE CITY OF CHICAGO, JUNE 1-3, 1887.

Indiana embraces an area of 33,809 square miles; has ninety-two counties, and a population (in 1880) of 1,978,301.

We are represented in this convention by our full quota, of sixty delegates, and probably a greater number of alternates; and these, in turn, represent many denominations,—among them, the Methodist Episcopal, Presbyterian, Friends, Baptist, Cumberland Presbyterian, Lutheran, Christian, Protestant Episcopal, Reformed, Congregational, German Baptist (Dunkard), United Brethren, Moravian, Mennonite, etc.—all working hold-of-hands in our Lord's Kingdom.

The Indiana Sunday School Union was organized in 1865, and has held state conventions, annually, ever since. We accomplished full county organization in 1877. During the year which closes with this date, we have held one or more county conventions in each and every of our ninety-two counties,—the whole number being one hundred and sixty-five; and beside these, district conventions have been held. On the pages following, we show the place and date of the *last* convention held in each county, (the next annual in Pike County is advertised for June 7, inst.) and the president and secretary of each county union.

We do not urge township organization—feeling that we have a plan better adapted to our country and time; yet very many township organizations are voluntarily maintained, and institutes regularly held;—one county of twelve townships held twenty-two institutes during the past year; and another of twelve townships, held twenty-eight institutes.

Indiana has performed all this work as a thank-offering to God,—never having paid a salary to any officer, in its prosecution, and no county has ever been organized, or its organization perpetuated, except by an assembly of its workers, called together for the purpose, by advertised notice. We gather statistics every year; and our efficient statistician exhibits an octavo volume, of ninety-two leaves—beside summary and index, which contains the reports from our ninety-two counties; and this form is in accord with our new and effective method of collecting, compiling, and preserving statistics. His detailed report is exhibited in a Chart displayed upon the wall of this auditorum ;—and shows, among other things, that Indiana has 4,498 Sunday-schools ; 46,898 Officers and Teachers ; 366,684 Scholars ; and, from 1,252 schools, (only 30 5-8 per cent. reporting,) has been received into church 21,680 ;—and we respectfully claim more of these to the square mile, and per population, than is possessed by any other state of material size. And we call attention to the fact, that our state has no large city to augment this per centage.

Indiana has paid all annual pledges to the International Sunday School Association, in regular semi-annual payments ; has paid all current expenses as they accrued, and has money in the Treasury.

JUNE 1, 1887.

CHAS. D. MEIGS, Jr. Treasurer.   WM. H. LEVERING. President.

JASPER FINNEY. Statistician.   CHAS. H. CONNER, Secretary.

District and County Organization:

With Place and Date of last County Convention, and name and address of District Presidents, and of the President and Secretary in each County.

DISTRICT.	COUNTY.	PLACE AND DATE.	PRESIDENT.	SECRETARY.
1 John F. Habbe, Evansville.	Vanderburg. Posey. Gibson. Pike.	Evansville, March 2-3, 1887 New Harmony,Mar.7-8, 1887 Princeton, May 26-27, 1887 Petersburg, May 25-26, 1886	Saml N. Curnick,Evansville A. H. Fretageot, N.Harmony A. J. Calkins, Princeton Rev. M. E. Chappell, Union	Fred Klein, Evansville Rev G D.Wolfe, N Harmony Miss J. Griffin, Princeton Miss M. M. Glezen, Peter-b'g
2 Wm. L. Wood, Huntingburg.	Warrick. Spencer. Dubois. Perry.	Boonville, Mar. 4-5, 1887 Rockport, May 28, 1887 Ireland, Oct. 21, 1886 Cannelton, May 7-8, 1887	Rev.JnoFerguson,Boonville John Wyttenbach,Rockport Clay Lemmon, Portersville Abel Powell, Cannelton	W. C. Hunton, Boonville Mrs.J.D. Armstrong,R'ckp't Mrs. S. Wineinger, Ireland Saml. L. Payne, Cannelton
3 Rev. E.P.Whallon, Vincennes.	Knox. Greene. Daviess. Martin.	Upper Indiana, Apl. 28, 1887 Worthington,Mar.17-18, 1887 Washington, Nov. 11, 1886 Shoals, May 10-11, 1887	R. McCord, Jr., Vincennes S. W. Axtell, Bloomfield N. H. Jepson, Washington Rev. Byram Carter, Shoals	Albert Fox, Vincennes Emma Hill, Bloomfield Hamlet Allen, Washington C. S. Wood, Loogootee
4 Wm. F. Osborn, Paoli.	Crawford. Harrison. Orange.	Marengo, Oct. 20, 1886 Corydon, Oct. 18-19, 1886 Broiner, May 19-20, 1887.	Prof.J.M.Johnson, Marengo Harry McGrain, Corydon John R. Simpson, Paoli	Rev. J. B. Rhodes, Milltown Miss Sallie K. Jones,Corydon H. G. Robbins, Lick Creek
5 D. M. Hammond, New Albany.	Floyd. Washington. Scott. Clarke.	New Albany, May 15, 1887 Pekin, May 17-18, 1887 Scottsburg, Apl. 26-27, 1887 Utica, Oct. 9, 1886	R. A. Ogg, New Albany Rev. I. L. St. John, Salem J. H. Friedley, Vienna Rev. W. R. Lathrop, Utica	H. A. Baldwin,New Albany Miss M. Trueblood, Salem J. B. Davis, Scottsburg N. G. Felker, Jeffersonville
6 Rev. Wm. Telfer, Bedford.	Lawrence. Monroe. Jackson.	Bedford, May 10-11, 1887 Smithville, May 24, 1887 Croths'ville, May 23-24, 1887	Wm. Tanksley, Mitchell Rev.W.B. Minton, Bl'm'gt'n Rev.M.E. M'Killip,Seymour	Mrs. E. E. Urner, Mitchell B.F.Adams,Jr.Bloomington Mrs. L.D. Carpenter,Seym'r